How To Develop & Market

Creative Business Ideas

By Dale A. Davis

The Oasis Press® / PSI Research
Grants Pass, Oregon

Published by The Oasis Press

How to Develop & Market Creative Business Ideas

© 1991 by Dale A. Davis

Edited by Scott Crawford
Editorial Assistance: Rosanno Alejandro, Wade Evans, Virginia Grosso,
Vickie Reierson
Page Formatting: Darrin Clay

Please direct any comments, questions, or suggestions regarding this book
to The Oasis Press, Editorial Department, at the address below.

The Oasis Press offers PSI Successful Business Software for sale.
For information, contact:
> PSI Research
> 300 North Valley Drive
> Grants Pass, OR 97526
> (503) 479-9464

The Oasis Press is a Registered Trademark of Publishing Services, Inc.,
a Texas corporation doing business in Oregon as PSI Research.

ISBN 1-55571-149-9 (paperback)

Printed in the United States of America
First edition 10 9 8 7 6 5 4 3 2 1   Revision Code: AAA

It is not the critic who counts,

not the man who points out how the strong man stumbled

or where the doer of deeds could have done them better.

The credit belongs to the man who is actually in the arena;

whose face is marred by dust and sweat and blood;

who strives valiantly;

who errs and comes short again and again;

who knows the great enthusiasms,

the great devotions,

and spends himself in a worthy cause;

who, at best, knows the triumph of high achievement,

and who, at the worst, if he fails,

at least fails while daring greatly,

so that his place shall never be

with those cold and timid souls

who know neither victory nor defeat."

Theodore Roosevelt
April 23, 1917

Ode To An Inventor

You have an idea and must give it a try,

You have a need to create and see your concepts fly;

You work out the bugs and create a little joy,

You act like a kid with a brand new toy;

You try every option and use every trick,

You are determined and won't be licked;

You know this business is not easy, and wonder why you dare,

You, my friend, are an inventor, so let the world beware.

Dedication

I dedicate this book to Wendy, my four-year-old daughter, a very special young lady whose imagination and enthusiasm has allowed me to see the world again through the curiosity and wonder of a child's eyes.

The awe and astonishment that shows in her eyes every day allows me to see that, without the preconceived notions of what can't be done, anything is possible, and life is endless in its wonder.

About the Author

Dale A. Davis is an inventor with a diversified background in engineering, industrial design, product design, packaging design, research and development, and entrepreneurial activities.

Mr. Davis licensed his first invention internationally by age 30 and has since been a consultant to, and an officer and principal of, a number of international companies.

Today the author continues his involvement with new product design and inventors through his seminars and Quest International, an organization Mr. Davis formed to help inventors and companies alike in the areas of patents, trademarks, copyrights, marketing, development of new product lines, and research.

Mr. Davis is a past chairman of the Oklahoma Inventors Congress and served on its State Board of Directors.

Acknowledgment

A sincere thank you to all who have given their time and encouragement to this book and especially to my wife, Angie, whose typing and editing allowed me to think about writing.

I am very fortunate to share in the dreams and creative passion of so many wonderful people.

Table of Contents

Introduction

I have always had the facility to dream up new ideas. I can't remember a time in my life when I wasn't dreaming about something; in fact, my dreaming has become an important part of my life.

When I decided I wanted to be an inventor (a career well suited for dreamers), I discovered dreams alone would never be enough. In order to see their visions take flight, dreamers, inventors, and most enterprising people need more. They need to be marketers, researchers, patent agents, financiers, model makers, production specialists, advertisers, brokers, and just plain lucky.

So begins the challenge. If you have an idea and you are determined to get your idea to market, you will have to acquire knowledge of each of these skills and more. If you're enterprising and creative and you have the courage to endure, then your dream, new idea, or concept is only the beginning of an adventure – an adventure filled with battles to fight, mountains to climb, and seemingly impossible obstacles to overcome.

You could even imagine your adventure in developing and marketing your idea as being similar to a medieval knight fighting dragons or on a holy quest. The only difference is that self-confidence is your lance, and knowledge and determination are your armor. If you are to be beaten, it's doubt, inexperience, and lack of knowledge that represent today's dragons.

As a self-taught entrepreneur and inventor, I strongly believe in doing as much as possible yourself. If you put yourself to the test of learning new skills, you'll greatly improve your chances of success. If you believe you can, half the battle is won. You may be able to hire experience, but you can't hire desire. It is much easier to give instructions than it is to convey your feelings about that idea or dream. I am not saying that you have to become an expert in every field –

sometimes it is beneficial to hire professionals during certain phases of development. I am, however, suggesting that you can learn to do much of what's needed to promote your own success, and that matched with a dream will, in the long run, be worth a lot more to you than any skilled professional (who you may not be able to afford anyway).

This book can be both teacher and guide for the adventure ahead. We will examine both the talent and resources needed. There is, however, one thing I cannot give you, and that's the motivation and determination you will have to get from within. I strongly believe that the power of a dream is unmatchable and that with a winning idea and determination, you will succeed.

Good teachers can point the way and share their experiences with others. I understand that what works for some people, however, does not necessarily work for others. Whatever I say in this book is based upon my own experience and the experience of hundreds of other inventors, business people, and entrepreneurs I have worked with. These experiences are meant to guide you, but your own insight and ability will often show you new paths which may even be better suited for you.

Part of the great adventure about creating and developing new ideas and dreams is the freedom to experiment and explore. You may decide to play it safe or risk all in your quest for success, but the decision has to be yours. And only you will feel the way an inventor feels when success is finally yours. Many inventors will fail on their first invention, only to learn from their experience and succeed with their next idea. The experience of a failed attempt should never be considered a failure, because the experience you gain will follow you for the rest of your life. Remember, Thomas Edison came up with hundreds of wrong ways to make a light bulb before he finally succeeded. For the dreamer who's not afraid to fail, there is a spirit inside which will not let you stay down, no matter what. Before you know it, another adventure is on its way and you're seeking more dragons to slay.

What's Ahead

If necessity is the mother of invention, then perseverance is the father. It's a long journey from dream to success, with many ups and downs along the way. So know where you're going and plan ahead. If you just want to "tinker," the experience is the reward, but most would probably like some financial rewards as well. Taking an idea to market must be managed as if it were a business, and as such, your business will have to be marketable if you're going to be successful for any length of time.

Once you've defined your idea, and even your purpose or goal, and believe that the idea does have a market, then it's time to get to work profiting from that idea. Before you start raking in the money, though, you must create a prototype, work out the "bugs," and consider different types of protection for your innovation. You must research, market, finance, and even license it. And that's where it gets interesting. In this book, we will approach each stage, learn about it, and utilize it. I have tried to leave no stone unturned, and yet I know I can't answer every question. I can offer you experience and knowledge, and if you provide insight and determination, success is possible.

How to Use This Book

The purpose of this book is to assist and guide the new entrepreneur, inventor, or creative thinker through the different processes which take an idea from conception to market. Before the idea becomes worth anything and the dream becomes reality, there are steps which must be taken along the way. Without these steps, ideas usually go nowhere. Many creative people will need guidance in many marketing and development areas, because often our creative nature does not prepare us for the world of business; that's what this book is all about. It explains each stage you will need to go through and, hopefully, provides some inspiration to try out your ideas.

Another reason for this book is that I remember my own experience starting out, and how I found no help or inspiration. The knowledge and resources are here for you to use. Use this book as a reference tool or as an instruction manual, but use it. The experience of hundreds of inventors, clients, and associates, as well as my own experience of taking products to market, are all within these pages. If you supply the necessary determination, the next success story may be yours.

About Pronouns

Masculine pronouns are used throughout this book, and is done for ease-of-reading purposes only. Attempts to use both masculine and feminine pronouns resulted in awkward sentence structure. Therefore, masculine pronouns are used with the understanding that they are intended as generic pronouns.

Chapter 1

Ideas

There are some people who look at life differently than most. Often these people are entrepreneurs, inventors, or otherwise creative, and they always seem to have a dream. These people are driven by a desire which only they can fully understand, but most of all they're dreamers.

Dreamers of the past, present, and future all share a special kinship; their dreams are an important part of creativity and innovative ideas – ideas which benefit everyone. Thomas Edison was a dreamer. He dreamed of a longer lasting lamp that could be operated by electricity. He believed in this innovation, and despite thousands of failures, his dream became reality. The lazy and indifferent will never see dreams come true. Only the ambition that comes from our own desire will turn dreams into reality.

Almost everyone is born with an inquiring and active mind, full of wonder and curiosity. My four-year-old daughter, Wendy, has a sense of wonder with the world which I truly envy. To be awed by the world around us, when most take it for granted, is surely a gift we lose all too soon by growing older.

But for the inventor or entrepreneur starting a new business or developing an idea, some of that wonder remains. That's why we still dream and believe that we can make a difference. The trouble is, dreams do not pay the bills – ideas are not tangible, and therefore are worth little if not developed. In the business world, only profits count. There will be no one applauding your efforts to improve life. The rewards you get will come from seeing your ideas become successes. Then the rewards will come in more ways than you can count.

Over the past 10 years, 73% of new industries were created by more than 12 million entrepreneurs with a dream. These dreamers were responsible for 40% of the country's gross national product and 86% of the new jobs created in the private sector. These same entrepreneurs produce 24 times as many innovations as large corporations. Yet for every success, there are hundreds of failures that we never hear about.

Failure is not a topic many like to talk about. No one writes books about or rewards failure, and yet most successes result from earlier failures. We may all like the inspiration we receive from hearing success stories, but we learn the most from experiencing failure. So don't expect quick success just because you have a dream – it won't happen. Your idea or concept will be tested time and time again; your chances of passing the test will depend on your determination and willingness to learn and adapt. Then you'll be headed in the right direction. I would rather say I've tried than ask, "I wonder if I could have been a success?"

Starting a File

If you're really going to take your idea to market or develop your dream further, you must get in the habit of working with your invention, idea, or new business concept in an organized manner.

The first thing to do is start a file. If you do not have a file cabinet or can't get one, use a shoe box or something else to hold all your papers, etc. having to do with your idea, and put everything that has to do with your idea in one place.

If you're one of those inventors who have literally hundreds of ideas and are still coming up with more, start another file for those other current ideas and future projects, and set it aside. Most importantly, pick one idea, and only one. Developing an idea for the market is hard enough without distractions.

The first item to file is a written description of your idea.

Defining Your Idea

You need to define your idea in writing. This may not be as simple as it sounds. If a certain process is required to make your invention, research the process; explain the reason for that particular process and why similar processes will not work. Chapter 3, which examines prototyping, will help you with this and even explain the different processes available to you. Write out why you feel your creation is better than existing products, and list its features and advantages.

What Is It?

In defining your idea, for example, don't just say that it's a plastic part. Explain what kind of plastic is used and why. Who have you talked with to determine which plastic should be used? Have you compared polyethylene to polypropylene? Do you know the price per pound of each plastic and its properties? To help you with the details, obtain a catalog from a plastics company; most such catalogs will have plastics properties charts in the back. I'm using plastic only as an example – all materials should be treated in the same way.

Defining your idea serves a couple of different purposes. Many inventors and creative thinkers have a tendency to let others worry about the details, even when those details are the obstacles which may keep the idea from the market.

Another purpose for defining your idea lies in the knowledge you will gain by having to understand a process well enough to explain it. Many times we think of a plastic part as being very inexpensive, not realizing that the tooling cost, set-up charges, and raw stock can cost thousands of dollars up front. A project I'm presently working on involves a plastic part that will cost five cents, but over $10,000 will be spent to produce that 5-cent part. The cost of tooling is often added into the manufacturing cost, thus increasing its retail cost.

Understanding these circumstances could help you determine how to develop and market your new idea.

What Does It Do?

In addition to defining what your invention is, you must also define what it does. The same fine detail should be used here as in your definition. When writing out what it does, you should also explain why other means will not work as well. Why should someone use your product and not someone else's? What are the advantages of using your product? How does your product really stand up to the competition?

Who Will Use It?

As long as you're listing all of this information, also list the potential customer. It's not as simple as merely stating that everyone will use the product – indicate how people are going to find out about it. Are they going to read about your idea in a magazine, or are they going to see it on television? Do you know what it's going to cost to advertise? Write to various media (newspaper, magazine, radio, television) to obtain information on advertising rates.

How Is It Unique?

By the time you have recorded all the details about your idea, you will probably find yourself more knowledgeable about your idea than before you started the written definition. Do the features still hold up against the competition? The market will be a tough place, and you need to be competitive. Your product has to be unique to really stand out. Considering that most advertising is written, you understand the importance of a complete, accurate written description.

Making an Objective Evaluation

One of the most difficult tasks any creative person can be asked to do is evaluate his own idea. Much like calling your own baby ugly, it just can't be done. Calling on friends to assist won't help because even a true friend would not necessarily tell you that your idea will not work. When it comes to the real market, there are no friends to buy your product. If it's a bad idea, you need to know now, while corrections can still be made.

If you take your idea to 20 strangers and they all hate it, you have an objective opinion that may help you create an even better new product. Remember, you can always improve on an idea; in fact, that's what got you into this in the first place. However, having a good idea does not mean the market is ready for it. Many creative people have come up with ideas ahead of their time. Some take years to develop and market while others literally become an overnight success.

There are no perfect ideas. There are bad ideas which made it to the market and good ideas still in someone's closet. The reason for an objective evaluation at this point is so all your energy will be spent in the right direction.

Additional information about inventors and developing ideas can be obtained by joining or visiting an inventors' organization in your area. The following, although not all inclusive, does list some of the major associations in various states.

Inventors' Organizations

ALABAMA

Alabama Inventors' Association
3409 Fountain Circle
Montgomery, AL 36116

ALASKA

Alaska Inventorprises
205 E. 4th Avenue
Anchorage, AK 99501

Alaskan Inventors' Office
P.O. Box 241274
Anchorage, AK 99524

Inventors' Institute of Alaska
P.O. Box 1327
Wassilla, AK 99587

ARKANSAS

Arkansas Inventors' Congress, Inc.
Route 3, Box 670
Dardanelle, AR 72334

CALIFORNIA

Inventors' Workshop
International Education Foundation
3201 Corte Malpaso, Suite 304-A
Camarillo, CA 93010

National Inventors' Foundation
345 W. Cypress Street
Glendale, CA 91204

CALIFORNIA (continued)

National Congress of Inventors' Organizations
214 Rheem Boulevard
Moraga, CA 94556

Inventors of California
215 Rheem Boulevard
Moraga, CA 94556

Inventors' Assistance League
345 W. Cypress Street
Glendale, CA 91204

Inventors' Council of California
250 Vernon Street
Oakland, CA 94610

California Inventors' Council
P.O. Box 2036
Sunnyvale, CA 94087

Inventors' Resource Center
P.O. Box 5105
Berkeley, CA 94705

Technology Transfer Society
11720 W. Pico Boulevard
Los Angeles, CA 90064

Silicon Valley Entrepreneurs Club, Inc.
TECHMART Building, Suite 3241
5201 Great America Parkway
Santa Clara, CA 95054

COLORADO

Affiliated Inventors' Foundation, Inc.
2132 E. Bijou Street
Colorado Springs, CO 80909

Governor's High Tech Cabinet Council
3271 S. Clay
Englewood, CO 80110

National Inventors' Cooperative Association
P.O. Box 6585
Denver, Co 80206

Rocky Mountain Inventors' Congress
P.O. Box 4365
Denver, CO 80204

CONNECTICUT

Inventors' Association of Connecticut
9 Sylvan Road South
Westport, CT 06880

FLORIDA

Society of American Inventors
2688 E. Fowler Avenue
Tampa, FL 33612

Tampa Bay Inventors' Council
P.O. Box 2254
Largo, FL 34649

Florida Entrepreneurship Program
Bureau of Business Assistance
Division of Economic Development
Florida Department of Commerce
107 W. Gaines Street, Room G-26
Tallahassee, FL 32399-2000

The Inventors Club
1000 College Boulevard
Pensacola, FL 32504

Society for Inventors and Entrepreneurs
306 Georgetown Drive
Casselberry, FL 32707

Central Florida Inventors' Council
P.O. Box 13416
Orlando, FL 32859

Innovative Products Group
2325 Ulmerton Road, Suite 16
Clearwater, FL 33520

FLORIDA (continued)

Palm Beach Society of American Inventors
P.O. Box 26
Palm Beach, FL 33480

Florida Product Innovation Center
One Progress Boulevard
Alachua, FL 32806

Innovation Product Group (IGP)
2325 Ulmerton Road, Suite 16
Clearwater, FL 33520

GEORGIA

Inventors' Club of America
P.O. Box 450261
Atlanta, GA 30345

Patent Assistance Program
Georgia Institute of Technology
Atlanta, GA 30332-0999

Inventors' Association of Georgia
241 Freyer Drive NE
Marietta, GA 30060

HAWAII

Inventors' Council of Hawaii
P.O. Box 27844
Honolulu, HI 96827

Statewide Strategy for High Technology Growth
High Technology Development Corporation
220 S. King Street, Suite 840
Honolulu, HI 96813

IDAHO

Idaho Research Foundation, Inc.
University of Idaho
P.O. Box 9645
Moscow, ID 83853

ILLINOIS

Inventors' Council of Chicago
53 W. Jackson, Suite 1041
Chicago, IL 60604

Illinois Business Innovation Fund
Illinois Department of Commerce and Community Affairs
100 W. Randolph Street, Suite 3-400
Chicago, IL 60601

Chicago High Tech Association
53 W. Jackson Boulevard, Suite 1634
Chicago, IL 60604

Technology Commercialization Center
Illinois State University
Normal, IL 61761-6901

Technology Commercialization Program
University of Illinois at Chicago
815 W. Van Buren Street
Chicago, IL 60607

INDIANA

Indiana Inventors' Association, Inc.
P.O. Box 2388
Indianapolis, IN 46206-2388

The Inventors and Entrepreneurs Society of Indiana, Inc.
P.O. Box 2224
Hammond, IN 46323

International Association of Professional Inventors
Route 10
Anderson, IN 46011

IOWA

Inventure
Drake University
210 Aliber Hall
Des Moines, IA 50311

KANSAS

Kansas Technology Enterprise Corporation
112 W. 6th, Suite 400
Topeka, KS 66603

Kansas Association of Inventors, Inc. (KAI)
2015 Lakin
Great Bend, KS 67530

KENTUCKY

Alternative Energy Development Program
Division of Alternative Energy Development
Kentucky Energy Cabinet
P.O. Box 3249
Frankfort, KY 40601

Center for Entrepreneurship
School of Business
University of Louisville
Louisville, KY 40292

LOUISIANA

Louisiana Innovation Program
Louisiana Department of Commerce
P.O. Box 94185
Baton Rouge, LA 70804

Technology Innovation Center
University of Southwestern Louisiana
P.O. Box 44172
Lafayette, LA 70504-4172

MAINE

Center for Innovation and Entrepreneurship
University of Maine
Maine Tech Center
16 Godfrey Drive
Orono, ME 04473

MARYLAND

Systems Engineering Center
University of Maryland
College Park, MD 20740

MASSACHUSETTS

Inventors' Association of New England
P.O. Box 335
Lexington, MA 02173

Innovation Invention Network
132 Sterling Street
West Boylston, MA 01583

Innovation Invention Network
132 Breakneck Road
Southbridge, MA 01550

Small Business Development Center
University of Lowell Research Foundation
450 Aiken Street
Lowell, MA 01854

MICHIGAN

Inventors' Council of Michigan
2727 Second Avenue
Detroit, MI 48201

Inventors' Center of Michigan
Ferris State University
1020 E. Maple Street
Big Rapids, MI 49307

MINNESOTA

Minnesota Inventors' Congress
P.O. Box 71
Redwood Falls, MN 56283-0071

Minnesota Project Innovation, Inc.
1107 Hazeltine Boulevard
Chaska, MN 55318

Midwest Inventors' Society
P.O. Box 335
St. Cloud, MN 56301

Inventors and Technology Transfer Society
P.O. Box 14775
Minneapolis, MN 55414

MINNESOTA (continued)

Society of Minnesota Inventors
20231 Basalt Street NW
Anoka, MN 55303

Rolling Inventors' Education Network
P.O. Box 14775
Minneapolis, MN 55414

MISSISSIPPI

Mississippi Research and Development Center
3825 Ridgewood Road
Jackson, MS 39211-6453

Confederacy of Mississippi Inventors
4759 Nailor Road
Vicksburg, MS 39180

Mississippi Society of Scientists and Inventors
P.O. Box 2244
Jackson, MS 39205

Mississippi Inventors' Workshop
4729 Kings Highway
Jackson, MS 39206

Society of Mississippi Inventors
P.O. Box 5111
Jackson, MS 39296

MISSOURI

Inventors' Association of St. Louis
P.O. Box 16544
St. Louis, MO 63105

Columbia Venture Club
Missouri Ingenuity, Inc.
T-16 Research Park
Columbia, MO 65211

Innovation Institute
Box 184
Route 2
Everton, MO 65646

Missouri Inventors' Association
204 E. High Street
Jefferson City, MO 65101

MONTANA

Montana Science and Technology Alliance
46 N. Last Chance Gulch, Suite 2B
Helena, MT 59620

Montana Inventors' Association
RR #1, Box 37
Highwood, MT 59450

Yellowstone Inventors' Association
P.O. Box 23306
Billings, MT 59104

NEBRASKA

Lincoln Inventors' Association
5201 Bluff Road
Lincoln, NE 68514

Omaha Inventors' Club
U.S. Small Business Administration
11145 Mill Valley Road
Omaha, NE 68145

Kearney Inventors' Association
Kearney Development Council
2001 Avenue A
Box 607
Kearney, NE 68847

NEVADA

Nevada Innovation and Technology Council
1755 E. Plum Lane, Suite 152
Reno, NV 89502

Nevada Chapter – Inventors' Workshop International
P.O. Box 9905
Reno, NV 89701

NEW JERSEY

National Society of Inventors
539 Laurel Place
South Orange, NJ 07079

American Society of Inventors
402 Cynwyd Drive
Absecon, NJ 08201

NEW MEXICO

The Genesis Center
New Mexico State University
P.O. Box 30001
Dept. 3RED
Las Cruces, NM 88003-0001

NEW YORK

New York Society of Professional Inventors
SUNY–College of Technology at Farmingdale
Lupton Hall
Farmingdale, NY 11735

Innovation Design Fund, Inc.
866 United Nations Plaza
New York, NY 10017

Center for Technology Transfer
SUNY–College at Oswego
209 Park Hall
Oswego, NY 13126

Pan Hellenic Society – Inventors of Greece in USA
2053 Narwood Avenue
South Merrick, NY 11566

NORTH CAROLINA

North Carolina Technology Development Authority
4216 Dobbs Building
430 N. Salisbury Street
Raleigh, NC 27611

NORTH DAKOTA

Innovation Institute
Box 429
Larimore, ND 58215

Center for Innovation and Business Development
University of North Dakota
Box 8103 University Station
Grand Forks, ND 58202

OHIO

Ohio's Thomas Edison Program's Seed Development Fund
Ohio Department of Development
77 S. High Street
Columbus, OH 43266-0330

Ohio Department of Development
Division of Technological Development
30 E. Broad Street
P.O. Box 1001
Columbus, OH 43266-0101

Inventors' Club of Greater Cincinnati
18 Gambier Circle
Cincinnati, OH 45218

Inventors' Council of Dayton
140 E. Monument Avenue
Dayton, OH 45402

Columbus Inventors' Association
2480 East Avenue
Columbus, OH 43202

Akron/Youngstown Inventor Organization
1225 W. Market Street
Akron, OH 44313

Inventors' Connection of Greater Cleveland
P.O. Box 46254
Bedford, OH 44146

OHIO (continued)

Inventors' Network of Columbus
1445 Summit Street
Columbus, OH 43201

Inventors' Council for Greater Lorain County
1005 N. Abbe Road
Elyria, OH 44035

National Invention Center
146 High Street, Suite 206
Akron, OH 44308

Ohio Inventors' Association
10595 Sand Ridge Road
Millfield, OH 45761

OKLAHOMA

Oklahoma Inventors' Congress
P.O. Box 54625
Oklahoma City, OK 73147

Invention Development Society
8502 SW 8th Street
Oklahoma City, OK 73128

Rural Enterprises, Inc.
P.O. Box 26980
Oklahoma City, OK 73126

OREGON

Western Inventors' Council
P.O. Box 3288
Eugene, OR 97403

Western Inventors' Council
E.E. Easton School of Business
Oregon State University
Corvallis, OR 97331

PENNSYLVANIA

American Society of Inventors
P.O. Box 58426
Philadelphia, PA 19102-8426

American Society of Inventors
545 Hughes Road
King of Prussia, PA 19406

American Society of Inventors
1710 Fidelity Building
123 South Broad Street
Philadelphia, PA 19109

SOUTH CAROLINA

Emerging Technology Development and Marketing Center
Clemson University
338 University Square
Clemson, SC 29634-5703

SOUTH DAKOTA

South Dakota Inventors' Congress
P.O. Box 1113
Watertown, SD 57201

TENNESSEE

Tennessee Inventors' Association
P.O. Box 11225
Knoxville, TN 37939-1225

Appalachian Inventors' Group
P.O. Box 388
Oak Ridge, TN 37830

Tennessee Inventors' Association
1116 Weisgarber
Knoxville, TN 37919

TEXAS

Technology Business Development
Texas Engineering Experiment Station
Texas A & M University
310 Wisenbaker Engineering Research Center
College Station, TX 77843-3369

TEXAS (continued)

Texas Innovation Information Network System
INFOMART
P.O. Box 471
1950 Stemmons Freeway
Dallas, TX 75207

Texas Inventors' Association
4000 Rock Creek Drive, Suite 100
Dallas, TX 75204

Innovex, Inc.
4144 N. Central Expressway
Dallas, TX 75204

Network of American Inventors and Entrepreneurs
402 Pierce, Suite 300
Houston, TX 77002

UTAH

Utah Technology Finance Corporation
419 Wakara Way, Suite 215
Salt Lake City, UT 84108

Intermountain Society of Inventors and Designers
5770 Minder Drive
Salt Lake City, UT 84121

VIRGINIA

Technology Commercialization Center for Innovation Technology
CIT Building, Suite 600
2214 Rock Hill Road
Herndon, VA 22070

Virginia Tech Corporate Research Center
Virginia Polytechnic Institute and State University
1800 Kraft Drive
Blacksburg, VA 24060

WASHINGTON

Innovation International Project
P.O. Box 4636
Rolling Bay, WA 98061

Inventors' Association of Washington, Inc.
P.O. Box 1725
Bellevue, WA 98009

Northwest Inventors' Association
723 E. Highland Drive
Arlington, WA 98223

WISCONSIN

Midwest Inventors' Group
P.O. Box 1
Chippewa Falls, WI 54729

Wisconsin Innovation Service Center
University of Wisconsin-Whitewater
402 McCutchan Hall
Whitewater, WI 53190-1790

For an updated list of all U.S. inventors' organizations, contact:

The National Institute for Inventors
P.O. Box 1465
Seneca, SC 29679

**The Argonne National Laboratory's
Study of Innovative Programs for Inventors**
Environmental Systems Division
Mail Stop 362-2B
Argonne, IL 60439

There are also governmental organizations that can help you by giving independent evaluations and assistance. These include:

National Innovation Workshop (NIW)
Office of Energy Related Inventions
National Institute of Standards and Technology
Gaithersburg, MD 20899

NIWs are inventors' seminars given throughout the country on such topics as patents, licensing, marketing, raising money, and sources of assistance.

SCORE (Service Corps of Retired Executives)
U.S. Small Business Administration
1441 L Street NW, Room 100
Washington, DC 20416
SCORE is comprised of retired executives who offer sound advice based on their years of experience.

NASA
Technology Utilization Programs
P.O. Box 8756
Baltimore, MD 21240

Office for Promoting Technical Innovation
New Jersey Department of Labor and Industry
Labor and Industry Building
Trenton, NJ 08625

National Technical Information Center
Springfield, VA 22161

Office of Energy Related Inventions
National Bureau of Standards
Gaithersburg, MD 20899

Army Materials and Mechanics Research Center
Watertown, MA 02172

Other sources to investigate:

Center for Innovation
P.O. Box 3809
Butte, MT 59701

Golden State Energy Center
Building 1055
Fort Cronkhite
Sausalito, CA 94965

University of Pennsylvania Small Business Development Center
The Wharton School
W-178 Dietrich Hall
Philadelphia, PA 19104

Office of the National Bureau of Standards
Institute of Applied Technology
Office of Energy-Related Inventions (OERI)
Department of Commerce
Washington, DC 20234

Science and Technology Division
Congressional Library
Washington, DC 20234

Office for the Advancement of Developing Industries
University of Alabama at Birmingham
University Station
Birmingham, AL 35294

Small Business Development Center
University of Alaska
430 W. 7th Avenue
Anchorage, AK 99501

Arizona State Research Institute
Arizona State University
Temple, AZ 85287

Entrepreneurial Service Center
University of Arkansas at Fayetteville
BA 443
Fayetteville, AR 72701

CONNECT, Program in Technology and Entrepreneurship
University of California at San Diego
X-001
La Jolla, CA 92093

Energy Technology Advancement Program
California Energy Commission
MS-43
1516 9th Street
Sacramento, CA 95814

American Inventors' Council
P.O. Box 4304
Rockford, IL 61110

Corporate Technology Sourcing
Baxter International
P.O. Box 490
Round Lake, IL 60073

EKMS, Inc.
106 Inman Street
Cambridge, MA 02139

Innovative Products Research and Services, Inc.
P.O. Box 335
Lexington, MA 02173

New Venture Research Corporation
10 South 5th, Suite 415
Minneapolis, MN 55402

Battelle Development Corporation
505 King Avenue
Columbus, OH 43201

Docie Marketing
10595 Sand Ridge Road
Millfield, OH 45761

The organizations listed below perform professional evaluations and will also provide assistance. If interested, write one of these agencies to find what type of assistance is available, and any costs involved.

Center for Research, Inc.
University of Kansas
2291 Irving Hill Road Campus
West Lawrence, KS 66045

Innovation Center
Massachusetts Institute of Technology
Room 33-111
Cambridge, MA 02139

Utah Innovation Center
University of Utah
417 Wakara Way
Salt Lake City, UT 84112

Center for Private Enterprise and Entrepreneurship
Hankamer School of Business, Suite 308
Baylor University
Waco, TX 76703

Wisconsin Innovation Service Center
University of Wisconsin
402 McCutchan Hall
Whitewater, WI 53190

Technology Commercialization Center
Illinois State University
Novey Hall 401L
Normal, IL 61761

Bureau of Business Research and Service
California State University at Fresno
Fresno, CA 93740

Center for New Business Executives
Innovation Center
P.O. Box 12793
Research Triangle Park, NC 27709

Technical Applications Center
University of New Mexico
Albuquerque, NM 87131

Innovation Information Center
George Washington University
2130 H Street NW
Washington, DC 20052

Bureau of Business and Economic Research
Jackson State University
1400 J.R. Lynch Street
Jackson, MS 39217

Bureau of Economic and Business Research
University of Illinois
408 David Kinley Hall
Urbana, IL 61801

Innovation Center
Stanford University
Stanford, CA 94305

Center for Entrepreneurial Development
Carnegie-Mellon University
4516 Henry Street
Pittsburgh, PA 15213

These are newsletters that deal with innovation:

International New Product Newsletter
6 St. James Avenue
Boston, MA 02116

Invention Management and Patent Newsletter
Communications Publishing Group
1505 Commonwealth Avenue
Boston, MA 02135

The Lightbulb Journal of the Inventors Workshop International
16218 Ventura Boulevard
Encino, CA 91436

New Product–New Business Digest
Business Growth Services
General Electric Company
120 Erie Boulevard
Room 308
Schenectady, NY 12345

New Product News
Dancer Fitzgerald Sample, Inc.
405 Lexington Avenue
New York, NY 10174

NOTES

NOTES

_____

_____

_____

_____

_____

_____

_____

_____

_____

_____

_____

_____

_____

_____

_____

_____

_____

_____

_____

_____

_____

_____

_____

_____

_____

_____

_____

Chapter 2

Patents, Trademarks & Copyrights

Introduction to Intellectual Property

Somewhere between your conception of a new idea and marketing your invention, you must investigate what form of protection you will need to obtain regarding your product. The decision will require an understanding of the many types of intellectual property.

Intellectual property is also referred to as intangible property, proprietary assets, industrial property or proprietary rights. Intellectual property covers patents, trademarks, copyrights, trade secrets, and trade names.

The laws that cover these topics are known as intellectual property laws, and, when necessary, are used in court to determine intellectual property rights. Intellectual property laws cover all forms of protection from patent infringements to unfair competition.

Defending Intellectual Property

Having intellectual property may mean you will someday have to defend your rights. Before the mid-1970s patents were deemed invalid in approximately 73% of the cases taken to court. This now seems to be changing in favor of the inventor.

Inventors, previously having only a 27% chance of their patents holding up in court, lost respect for patents. The lack of enforce-ability of U.S. patents resulted in a 34% decline in the number of patents awarded to Americans between 1972 and 1982.

Today, there are no criminal penalties for patent infringement; there are, however, the following civil remedies:

1. An injunction against future infringement.

2. Compensatory damages, in no event less than a reasonable royalty.

Some important changes that have taken place to help inventors include Congress' establishing a Federal Circuit Court of Appeals for patent matters.

The Federal Circuit Court has more expertise in the field of patents than it had in the past. As a result, more than half of the patent claims submitted to the court since 1985 have been held valid and lower court findings of patent validity have been affirmed more than 86% of the time.

Due to the decisions described below, infringers are less likely to litigate an infringement suit.

- In *Lemelson v. Mattel*, a jury found that Mattel had infringed on Lemelson's patent and awarded damages of $70 million.

- General Motors had to pay $8.8 million in damages and over $11 million in pre- and post-judgment interest for infringement on a lubricating process patent.

- Smith International was ordered to pay $205 million for infringing a Hughes Tool patent.

- One large damage case claimed that Kodak infringed upon seven Polaroid patents. Kodak's potential liability to Polaroid could exceed $1 billion.

- Ford Motor Company was found to have infringed on a patent on intermittent windshield wipers.

Before considering whether an infringement suit is warranted, consider that many cases will require years to complete and may proceed from the U.S. District Court to a U.S. Court of Appeals for the Federal Circuit, and may even be taken to the Supreme Court. The cost involved in such court proceedings can be staggering.

Although patents are often the subject of infringement suits, copyrights, trademarks, trade secrets, and unfair competition may also be subjected to the same proceedings.

The Basics for Idea Protection

Creating a paper trail is one of the oldest and most inexpensive ways of protecting your invention by documenting its date of conception.

One of the best ways of doing this is to obtain and use an inventor's log book. The ideal log book is bound or stitched so its pages cannot be removed because the pages must be used consecutively. A looseleaf notebook would not work. One easy way to start an inventor's log book is to purchase a daily planner at any stationery or business supply store and use it as a log.

The log book, properly maintained, can be used as documentation in the event of a legal dispute, and therefore should not be taken lightly. The inventor's log book should be started as soon as possible after the idea is conceived. Further, the inventor's log book is more than a means of effectively documenting the date of conception — it also serves you well in recording test results, successful prototypes, and failures.

A well-kept log book will include your thoughts, sketches, notes, calculations, telephone numbers, and contacts.

In order for the log book to stand up in court, it is advisable to document everything so that anyone reading it can easily understand and comprehend the information. Remember, once an invention is described in detail, you should date and sign the appropriate page or pages, and have your signature notarized or witnessed.

If it seems risky to have your log book notarized, remember that the notary is merely witnessing your signature and the date, and does not need to see or understand the information contained in your log book regarding your invention. Although keeping a log book and having it notarized occasionally may seem somewhat troublesome, the log book's ultimate importance will be determined by your invention's possibilities and your diligence in maintaining it properly.

Even if you never have to use your log book for legal matters, its importance cannot be understated or diminished. Sometimes going back six months in the log book to locate an old telephone number or contact can have real value in itself.

Guidelines for Maintaining a Log Book

These guidelines will help you maintain a quality log book:

1. Keep a separate log book for each project you work on, and make notes each time you work on your invention.

2. Once your idea is developed to some potential, describe it and have the description notarized or witnessed.

3. Keep all records such as telephone numbers, contacts, addresses, notes, tests, and any reference material in your log book.

4. Do not leave blank pages. Use your log book chronologically to maintain its validity.

5. When demonstrating a prototype to a witness, have the witness give a written description of the operation and the results observed. The witness should then sign and date the appropriate page or pages.

Keeping a log book is a common practice of engineers, designers, and research and development personnel who want to maintain clear and accurate records of the genesis and progress of their ideas.

Disclosure Document Program

The disclosure document program is for the inventor who wishes to obtain alternative or additional protection.

The program is administered by the U.S. Patent and Trademark Office, which accepts and preserves your invention disclosure document in strict confidence for a period of two years, or longer if your patent application refers to the disclosure. The purpose of this service is to provide a credible form of evidence, should you need it. Originally, this service was intended to stop inventors from mailing a description of their own inventions to themselves, which they believe to be a valid form of protection — it is not.

The disclosure document is not a substitute for a patent application and should not be considered a grace period for filing the application. The program is aimed at allowing inventors to feel protected enough to proceed with their ideas, rather than hiding or sitting on them. Just like an inventor's log book, a disclosure document can be upheld in court and can ultimately resolve a patent infringement case.

Filing a Disclosure Document

The method for filing a disclosure document is as follows:

1. Send, on an $8^1/2$ by 11 sheet of paper (or a copy from your log book) a description of your invention. The description is important. It must be limited to written matter or drawings on paper or other thin, flexible material such as linen, plastic, or Mylar, having dimensions or folded to dimensions not to exceed $8^1/2$ by 13 inches.

2. Number each page. Text and drawings should be sufficiently dark and bold to permit reproduction with commonly used office copying machines. Photographs may be submitted, but they are not required. Although not a requirement, you may want to have the disclosure document notarized.

3. Send your description, along with a check or money order for $6 payable to the Commissioner of Patents and Trademarks, to the address shown below. Include a stamped, self-addressed envelope and this signed request in duplicate:

"The undersigned, being the inventor of the disclosed invention, requests that the enclosed papers be accepted under the disclosure document program and that they be preserved for a period of two years."

Sign the request and mail, along with the description, to:

Commission of Patents and Trademarks
Washington, DC 20231

When received by the Patent and Trademark Office, your disclosure document will be stamped with an identification number and the date of receipt. The duplicate request will then be returned to you in the self-addressed envelope together with a notice indicating that the disclosure document may be relied upon only as evidence, and that a patent application should be filed if patent protection is desired. The disclosure document program does not diminish the value of your notarized and witnessed records as evidence of the conception date of your invention; it does, however, provide the Patent and Trademark Office with a credible form of evidence which can be referred to in a separate letter in the patent application, should you decide to file within the two-year period.

Patents

A patent is a grant that results from a contract with the U.S government, whereby the inventor agrees to disclose his invention to the public in order to further technology. In return, the government grants the inventor the right to exclude all others from making and selling the product for a certain period of time.

History of Patents

Patent law in the United States has an interesting history, which began in 1790 when the first patent laws were adopted.

Our forefathers recognized the need to protect new ideas, and created a specific provision authorizing a grant of protection for a limited time to authors and inventors.

This provision, Article 2, Section 8, became effective March 4, 1789, and was implemented April 10, 1790, by George Washington, thus giving Congress the power to promote the useful arts.

Since then, the laws have changed a number of times. One important change came in 1952, allowing a patent to be issued for a new use of an old device. But the basic concept of providing an exclusive right to an inventor has always remained the same.

The United States was not the first nation to adopt such laws on patents. In fact, we can trace the historical development of patents back to ancient Greek and Roman times. The first patent in recorded history was granted in the ancient Greek colony of Sybusis in 500 B.C. for a gourmet dish. During the Dark Ages, patents seemed to disappear and very little innovation, if any, took place. However, during the latter part of the Middle Ages, procedures were again organized to protect inventors and improve technology.

In the 1300s, new ideas used in the design and construction of canals, bridges, and mills in Venice were protected. In 1330, France offered a royal degree to inventors for developing ideas and inventions.

By the year 1500, inventions and patents flourished in the Italian states and the German empire. Thereafter, the custom of granting patents was adopted in the Netherlands and England. From England, patents were extended into the American Colonies. Until 1790, patents were granted by a colony to its citizens. In receiving a patent, inventors obtained a grant from the U.S. government for a limited monopoly.

The first U.S. patent was issued on July 31, 1790, to Samuel Hopkins for a process for making "pot and pearl ashes."

The U.S. Patent Office, established in 1802, was initially operated under the Department of State. In 1849, the Patent Office was placed under the authority of the Department of the Interior, and in 1925, under the Department of Commerce. For the first 80 years the Patent Office required a working model of an invention in order to issue a patent.

Patents in General

A patent generally allows an inventor the right to exclude others from making and selling his product for 17 years, provided that maintenance fees are paid every $3^1/2$ years.

If maintenance fees are not paid after the first $3^1/2$ years, the patent becomes void and public domain. While patents are considered a grant or contract with the government, they actually offer no rights at all. Patents do offer the right to keep others from using or selling the patented invention, but they do not offer the monopoly many believe to coexist with patents. Patents are in a sense a license to litigate, or, in other words, a reason to sue.

Why, then, would anyone want to obtain a patent? To sue others? To keep infringers at bay? A patent will become a most expensive asset even if you win your lawsuits. If, instead, your reasons for patenting an invention or idea are to obtain protection and a marketing tool, you'll find that a patent can become a tremendous asset.

There are three types of patents available today: utility patents, design patents, and living plant patents.

Utility Patents

If your invention relates to a functional aspect of any machine, process, method, article, or composition, the best method of protection may be the utility patent.

Utility patents are by far the most common of all patents and protect everything from new machinery to genetically altered animals. There are some 400 different categories for utility patents, covering such items as hardware, toys, tools, vehicles, sporting goods, time- and labor-saving devices, and cooking implements.

With the exception of items covered by the Atomic Energy Act of 1954, which excludes the patenting of inventions used solely in the manufacture of nuclear or atomic weapons, nearly everything can be classed into the patent classification system. The patent classification system is discussed in further detail later in this chapter.

Design Patents

If you believe that your invention has a unique ornamental appearance and you would like to protect its external appearance, then a design patent is the way to go. Design patents are not only easier to apply for and receive, but are far less costly than a utility patent.

To be patentable as a design patent your invention's appearance must not be obvious – that is, someone with ordinary skills in your field would not easily design the same appearance. Because many past inventors have used design patents when their inventions did not qualify for a utility patent, design patents have an image of being somewhat weak in nature or second rate, but this is not true.

Design patents allow the same rights as a utility patent and allow you to use the patent pending status and to license your invention, as does a utility patent.

A design patent is only applicable to aesthetics or ornamental features; the design in itself may have no significant functional purpose. The design must be inseparable from the invention and cannot be a surface ornamentation, such as a cover or label.

A good example of a design that could be patented is a tire tread design. The tread offers a design feature to the tire, which by itself would be unpatentable. The design patent on the tread would protect your invention from infringers using any similar designs. Design patent applications consist of a drawing, appropriate forms, and a $125 filing fee if you are an individual inventor or small company.

Plant Patents

The Plant Patents Act of May 23, 1930, amended U.S. patent law to permit protection of any new and distinct variety of asexually reproduced plants, other than tuber-propagated plants. This legislation supported the plant breeders who are few in number, yet important to the advancement of agriculture.

Plant patents cover all new varieties of plants produced asexually from cutting and grafting and, unlike with utility patents, usefulness is not a requirement for patentability. One of the better known plant patents is for the peach, invented by Luther Burbank, who also invented the Burbank potato (introduced into Ireland to help combat the blight epidemic). Burbank invented more than 800 new strains of plums, prunes, berries, and lilies. Plant patents, though rare, are still very important to today's agricultural market.

Qualifying for a Patent

In discussing the patentability of your invention, consider this passage from United States Code Title 35-101 under "Inventions Patentable":

"Whoever invents or discovers any new and useful process, machine, manufacture, or composition of matter, or any new and useful improvement thereof, may obtain a patent thereof, subject to the conditions and requirements of this title."

Title 35-102 further dictates conditions for patentability, including:

1. The invention cannot be known or used by others, or patented or described in a printed publication anywhere before the inventor applies for a patent.

2. The invention cannot be used in public or be on sale for more than one year prior to application for a patent.

3. The invention cannot be abandoned in another application.

4. The invention cannot already be patented for more than one year in a foreign country.

5. The invention cannot be described in another patent or application.

6. The invention cannot be invented by someone else.

In determining the priority of inventions which have been filed at the same time, there shall be considered not only the respective dates of conception and the reduction to practice, but also the reasonable diligence of who was first to put the invention into practice.

This section shows that, should there be an interference in patents, the Patent Office will evaluate who actually did the most to commercialize the invention. The United States is the only country that awards patents to the first to conceive, not the first to patent.

Now that we've examined the requirements necessary for you to obtain a patent, it may be easier to understand what is not patentable:

- An idea, as opposed to a mechanical device;

- A method of doing business;

- Printed matter which you would copyright;

- Inoperable devices such as perpetual motion machines, without working prototypes;

- An obvious improvement, such as using plastic to replace steel;

- Illegal inventions such as a money-making machine or a new safe-cracking explosive;

- Nuclear weapons (hopefully, no one would worry about this);

- Theoretical matters, such as the Big Bang theory;

- Subject matter which falls under trademarks or copyrights; or

- Untested drugs, which require FDA approval to be patentable.

With these guidelines, it should now be much easier to determine if your idea is patentable.

How Long Do Patents Last?

Utility and plant patents are both granted for 17 years. In contrast, design patents last 14 years. Utility patents also require payment of maintenance fees every 3 to $3^1/2$ years to keep the patent in effect.

Only patents subject to regulatory review, such as those for drugs and food additives, can be extended beyond 17 years. This is due to a new federal statute, 35 USC 155-156.

How to Apply For a Patent

In order to obtain a patent, you must file an application with the federal government asking that it find the subject matter described in the application new, useful, and unobvious. Contact a patent agent to assist you in the preparation of a patent application; or, you can file one yourself, using one of the self-help books available. If you choose to do your own filing, I suggest reading:

> **Patent It Yourself**
> By David Pressman
> Published by Nolo Press
> 950 Parker St.
> Berkeley, CA 94710

A word of warning when filing for your own patent: Become knowledgeable about the process before you start, or you may place your patent at risk. This is not to say that you should not file for your own patent. I've filed all my own patents and believe the inventor is the best person to do so, providing he is serious enough to become knowledgeable in the matter.

Consider your morning cup of coffee. To you, it may simply be coffee, but to a patent examiner, it may be a precise combination of water, caffeine, ethanol, butanol, methyl acetaldehyde, methyl formate, dimethyl sulfide, propionaldehype, acetic acid, furfural, furfuryl alcipice, methyl acetate, methylfuran, and diacetyl isoprence.

Writing a patent application can be an art form all its own, and it should be well researched in order to be effective.

Patent Application Contents

A patent application consists of these items:

1. Specifications, including:

   a) The title of your invention

   b) Background or history of the invention

   c) The invention's features, advantages, and objectives

   d) A brief description of the drawings

  e) A narrative description of the structure

  f) An explanation of how the invention works

  g) A summary of claims

2. Drawings

3. A filing fee, either check or money order

4. A transmittal (cover) letter

5. A stamped, self-addressed receipt postcard

6. Forms, including:

  a) A completed Patent Application Declaration

  b) A Small Entity Declaration, if an individual or company has fewer than 500 employees

  c) An Information Disclosure Statement

  d) Copies of patents you cited in your application and listed on the Information Disclosure Statement.

The forms required for filing a patent application can be obtained from the Patent Office or the library's book of forms.

Patent Costs

Shown below and on the following page are the fees charged, as of November 5, 1990, by the U.S. Patent and Trademark Office for filing an application. The fees shown are for small businesses (fewer than 500 employees).

Filing Fees

Utility patent	$ 315
Design patent	$ 125
Plant patent	$ 210

Claims

Independent claims in excess of three	$ 30 each
Claims in excess of 20	$ 10 each
Multiple dependent claims	$ 100

Reissue Application Fee $ 315

Response Extension Fees
One month $ 50
Two months $ 150
Three months $ 365
Four months $ 575

Appeals and Hearings Fees
Notice of appeal $ 120
Brief in support of appeal $ 120
Oral hearing request $ 100

Issue Fees
Utility patent $ 525
Design patent $ 185
Plant patent $ 260

Maintenance Fees (utility patents only)
At $3^1/2$ years $ 415
At $7^1/2$ years $ 835
At 12 years $1,250

These fees are generally less than you may spend for a patent agent or attorney.

While fees vary nationwide, you can expect to pay a patent agent $1,000 to $3,500 for preparing your application. Patent attorneys, on the other hand, will charge you anywhere from $3,000 to $10,000 for the same preparation. There are also charges for the actual patent drawings; they range from $75 to $200 per drawing.

In some areas there are patent experts or consultants who will assist you in preparing your own patent application, and will usually charge less than $1,000 for their services.

But be careful to avoid con men in this profession. It may be wise to avoid the services found in the back of some supermarket tabloid and some of the so-called inventor assistance groups known for their 1-800 numbers publicized on late-night television. These services may end up costing you a great deal of money and accomplish little. Although it would be unfair to assume that all invention brokers are of questionable character, many are more concerned about profit from inventors than profit from inventions. Use common sense when choosing any business associate.

Time Requirements for Filing

In the United States there are several legal requirements before you can obtain a patent. One is that the application must be filed within one year after the invention is first placed in public use, disclosed in a printed publication, or placed on sale. If you do not file within a year, you will have lost your right to file.

Ownership of Patents

A patent application must originally be filed in the name of the actual inventor. However, patent rights may be assigned, licensed, or even given away. Assignments must be in writing and must be recorded in the U.S. Patent and Trademark Office within three months of the assignment. In an employment situation, if the employee is hired to invent specific subject matter, any patent obtained on such subject matter would be owned by the employer. Many employees sign contracts which specifically provide for ownership of all patent rights.

Foreign Patents

One hundred seventy-nine nations provide some form of patent protection for new inventions. Patent protection provided by many countries extends to their colonies, territories, and protectorates.

An example of this is U.S. patents, which are enforceable in Eastern Samoa, Guam, the Panama Canal Zone, Puerto Rico, and the Virgin Islands. If your product is headed to another country, a foreign patent may be a necessity.

Fortunately, a U.S. patent application preserves the right to file in a foreign country for a period of one year from the U.S. filing date. An application filed in the U.S. would give you a priority date if you were to obtain a foreign patent.

The United States and most nations are parties to patent protection treaties which provide reciprocal patent rights to their citizens. One important reciprocal right is the right of priority, whereby foreign patent applications are treated as having been filed on the dates of corresponding U.S. patent applications on which they are based. Thus, the U.S. filing date can be the effective filing date of most foreign patents applications filed within one year.

In the United States, the patent rights generally belong to the first inventor, but in most foreign countries they belong to the inventor with the earliest effective patent application. Filing a U.S. patent application usually results in another benefit, such as a foreign filing license. Shortly after you file your U.S. application, you will probably receive your foreign filing license which authorizes the filing of a foreign patent application. You can file a foreign patent before filing a U.S. patent. If you do, the one-year filing period runs from the date of the foreign application filing.

If you are interested in filing a foreign patent, you can save thousands of dollars by dealing directly with foreign patent agents. A problem you will encounter when dealing directly with another country will be finding a patent attorney in that country. Your library can help you here. Many libraries have the resources to help you get the listing you need. Another option would be to send your request by fax, thus avoiding excessive long distance phone bills.

One such patent agent service I have used with success is:

Wilson, Gunn Ellis & Co.
41-51 Royal Exchange
Cross Street
Manchester, England

When filing foreign patents, you should also consider regional patents. Regional patents can be filed with either the European Patent Organization (EPO) or the African Intellectual Property Organization (AIPO).

EPO patent applications cover Austria, Belgium, France, Germany, Greece, Italy, Luxembourg, Netherlands (Holland), Spain, Sweden, Switzerland, Liechtenstein, and the United Kingdom (England, Wales, Scotland, and Ireland). Although an application is examined by the EPO, each country within the organization issues its own patent.

AIPO patents protect your invention in Benin, Cameroon, Central African Republic, Chad, Congo, Gabon, Mali, Mauritania, Senegal, and Togo. Filing a single EPO or AIPO patent application can be much less expensive than filing individually in each country.

The formation of the EPO and AIPO can be attributed largely to the Patent Cooperation Treaty (PCT). In 1987, the United States adopted important provisions of the PCT which gave U.S. patent filers these advantages in filing foreign patents:

1. The final designation of the foreign countries in which patent coverage is desired can be delayed for up to 30 months after the U.S. filing date;

2. With the addition of Canada in 1989, most of the important industrialized nations are now members of the PCT;

3. Filing and prosecution of the early phases of a PCT application are entirely in English; and

4. A PCT patent application can be used to delay the issuance of a U.S. patent or to cause a U.S. application to be published early in the procedure.

While the PCT, AIPO, and EPO help American inventors, they also help foreign inventors obtain U.S. patents.

In 1989, all global regions increased the number of U.S. patents they received. Pacific Rim countries received 22,611 patents, up 25.3% over the previous year, with 20,907 going to the Japanese, the largest number issued to a foreign country.

West European countries accounted for the second largest number of patents with 22,159, up 16.7%, with the French inventors taking the largest share at 3,310 patents. East European inventors received 25.4% more patents in 1989 than in 1988. Even Third World countries accounted for a significant increase of 28.8%.

American inventors only last year reversed a steady 25-year decline by receiving 53.3% of U.S. patents, an increase of 24.2%. Californians received nearly twice as many patents as New Yorkers.

Patent Searches

It is always advisable to conduct a patent search prior to either retaining legal counsel or filing a patent application yourself. The patent search is your insurance against spending time and money unnecessarily. When doing your patent search, you will either become more aware of just how brilliant your idea really is, or you may find a dozen or more different versions of your idea already patented. Of course, finding similar prior art is not necessarily bad news. The education you get from reviewing other inventions should only assist you in further developing your own invention.

I highly recommend doing your own patent search. There are patent libraries in each state for doing your search, and the day spent searching and traveling could save you up to $500. A listing of your nearest patent library is included in this book.

If you really want to dive in head first, go to Arlington, Virginia, and do your search at the main patent library. The Arlington library contains approximately 28 million documents in the search file, with some 5 million of these being U.S. patents. Dating back to 1790 when the patent system began, this library boasts more than 9 million cross-references and more than 13 million foreign patent documents. In addition, there are more than 120,000 volumes of information in the scientific library, consisting of trade literature, texts, digests, and journals. There are more than 400 classes of inventions and 120,000 subclasses. Before actually doing your own patent search, you must weigh the considerations, and if you decide to go ahead, have your class and subclass in hand. This is discussed in the chapter section on the patent classification system. Be prepared to spend an entire day; I can guarantee you that it will be both interesting and educational.

If you are not able to get to your city library and use the manual of classification, or are not able to send in your request to the patent office, you can look up your class and subclass at the state and/or patent library, but these manuals are usually in short supply at patent libraries.

Once you have determined your class and subclass, find a patent librarian and request the computer listing of all patents in your class.

The computer listing, which may contain from 30 to 200 patents or more, generally comes from the main patent library in Arlington and will list the patents in which you need to search. The patents are listed chronologically, beginning with the newest patents.

The first thing you may question on your listing is the letters beside certain numbers: "D" indicates that the patent is a design patent; "X" indicates a cross reference; and "R.E" indicates a reissue.

Now, with a brief understanding of what you are looking for, you can start your search by examining the abstracts in the *Official Gazette*. The *Official Gazette* is published weekly and lists the patents issued for that week, grouped by general, mechanical, chemical, electrical, design, and reissued patents.

The *Official Gazette* offers a means for viewing a summary of the invention, known as an abstract. Along with the abstract there will also be a drawing, where possible. This abstract allows a more efficient search without your having to dig through the mountains of paperwork on the five million-plus U.S. patents.

The best way I have found to do your search is to look up each listed patent number from top to bottom in the *Official Gazette* and mark the patents of interest. After eliminating the patents which you feel are not relevant, make a list of those patents that you would like to more closely examine.

In many libraries you may give the librarian the list of relevant patents, and they will make copies of them, usually at a nominal charge. Many librarians may simply direct you to the patent files and copying machine to make your own copies. So be sure to take a pocket full of change. If cost is not an issue and you have the time, the list may also be sent to the Patent and Trademark Office for copies at the prevailing rates.

One word of warning when doing your search: The day may become quite long and you may find yourself scanning or even missing relevant patents. This may come back to haunt you later. So if you need a break, take one. Remember, it is easier to do it right the first time than make an additional trip later.

The Patent Classification System

The U.S. Patent and Trademark Office maintains a highly sophisticated classification system, arranging patents into more than 400 subject classes and more than 120,000 subclasses in chronological order dating back to 1790.

Without this system of classes and subclasses it would be impossible to make any kind of patent search. A typical class, such as fasteners, can have subclasses, further breaking fasteners down into nail, stapling or clenching fasteners, to further define and assist in doing a patent search.

Although searching 400 classes and 120,000 subclasses may seem somewhat mind-boggling, the research to find your class and subclass starts with a trip to the public library, to look through the *Patent Office Manual of Classification.* You can also purchase the manual in loose-leaf form, by writing to the Superintendent of Documents, U.S. Government Printing Office, Washington D.C. Because the patent classification system is so sophisticated, the Patent Office offers a free service to inventors to help find their class and subclass, but this service can take three to eight weeks before you would receive a response.

If you do choose to have the Patent Office classify your invention for you, show your name and address at the top of a $8^1/2$" x 11" sheet of paper. Below that write: "Please advise me what subject area and/or class(es) and/or subclass(es) cover my intended invention." Then list your invention's features, operation, and intended use. Give accurate details, so that your idea is fully understood; otherwise you may be given an incorrect class or subclass. Once completed, mail the information to:

Commissioner of Patents and Trademarks
Washington, D.C. 20231

Computer Searches

Another method of searching patents is through a computer database. Computer patent searches consist of keywords being searched through different databases to match topic matter.

Computer searches can be very effective for doing preliminary searches before going into a more thorough patent search. If you have a personal computer with a modem, or know someone with one, you can perform your own search. Be aware that these databases charge anywhere from $10 to $100 per hour; a typical search could cost you $40 to $100 per hour. The first search has a learning curve which will cost you extra money and time. Some services even assess additional service charges of $50 or more for first-time use.

Unless you wish to do several searches, your savings in time may not be worth the trouble and expense of doing the search. Computer searches will give you an abstract, but not a drawing, so consider the type of search you are doing before deciding if computer searching is for you.

If you decide that you would like to give computer searching a try, here are some patent search databases and their telephone numbers:

Dialog (claims) (800) 334-2564

Questel (800) 424-9600

Permagon (800) 336-7575

Bibliographic Research (800) 833-4707

Mead Data Central (Lexput) (800) 543-6862

Evaluating Your Search

The patent search can be a very humbling experience. It could be quite a surprise to discover that your "new" idea was in fact patented in 1892. Don't let similar patents discourage you. It would be nearly impossible to go through millions of patents and not find some similar prior art.

Any patents which are similar can later be turned into tools. I can still remember my own discouragement when doing my first search. I found out that my invention was 200 years old, yet still not on the market. This intrigued me so much that I improved my invention even further, using the 200-year-old patent, and decided I was going to put this idea on the market. Within a year, I had licensed my patent in three countries, using that 200-year old idea.

Look at the whole picture and use your search as a tool – not a crutch.

Patent Pending

Throughout discussions on the many aspects of patents, we've discussed very little about what's going on during the time you're applying for a patent, that stage between sending in the patent application and possibly receiving a patent.

The fact is, this stage of the adventure requires special considerations. If you are proceeding with the marketing of your invention, as you should be, the only legal protection you can obtain is the Patent Pending label. The Patent Pending label legally warns would-be patent infringers that a patent has been applied for and may be granted. If, however, you are tempted to use the Patent Pending label without first filing an application, you can be fined $500 for this federal offense.

If you have a patent, you have the right to take an infringer to court. If you have a patent pending, you have only the right to tell would-be infringers that when a patent is granted, you intend to take them to court. In order to get an infringer to court, you will have to bear the cost of an attorney and all court costs until you can prove guilt.

Any judgment to stop an infringer will provide damages equal to 50% of his or her earnings from your invention. The infringer's loss is usually only in the tooling used to produce your invention. Generally, infringers settle out of court by buying a license to continue producing your invention.

One thing to consider before taking an infringer to court is that a percentage of infringers will take the offensive and try to invalidate your patent. Your patent's validity can be questioned in court by finding prior art similar to yours which was not discussed in your application. And with five million patents to search through, the chances are there that something similar will be found.

The truth of the matter is, Patent Pending does not strike fear into the heart of the would-be infringer. Patent Pending is really aimed at keeping the honest company honest.

Patent pending is both a marketing tool and a bluff. You have no rights to stop others from making your invention while applying for a patent. You could write a letter to the would-be infringer and warn them that when you receive your patent, you will sue them. They could in fact write a similar letter to you after filing their own patent application. The point here is to put your faith in the invention and not the possible patent. If your plan is to license your invention, remember that an existing market has more bargaining power than a proposed patent.

While your invention is pending patent, explore the market, even if only in a limited fashion, and work on establishing a trademark, trade dress, marketing studies, and even licensing. One of my inventions was licensed before the patent application had ever been filed.

You need to consider the importance and potential of your invention far more than the potential of a patent. You will find when approaching the marketplace that your invention will evolve according to market influences. In some cases, the market influences the invention so much that the original patent is abandoned, and a new invention is created and patented.

Depending on the invention, new improvements needed for marketing your invention can even be incorporated into an existing patent application. During office actions, claims will be amended and strengthened, sometimes even allowing new subject matter, if done properly.

Trademarks and Service Marks

If your creation includes any written or artistic matter which includes a symbol, word, shape, or design, and you use this mark as a brand name, service mark, or trade dress, you qualify for protection under trademark law.

Trademarks are used by a manufacturer or merchant both to identify goods, and to distinguish them from those goods manufactured or sold by others.

A trademark can be obtained as easily as affixing the letters ™ to your mark, or you can register it with state or federal trademark offices.

Many people consider trademarks a brand name and will buy products based upon their former experiences with a certain trademark. Service marks are sometimes confused with trademarks, but are actually slogans or phrases used in the sale or advertising of services rather than products.

Service marks identify the services of one person or company and distinguish them from the services of others. For example, the use of the slogan "We print it in a minute" by a printing business indicates the type of services rendered to its customers. Service marks and trademarks are registered in the same way.

A trademark only protects you from someone using a similar mark, which could cause confusion, on his goods. A trademark of an anchor for a line of boats could in fact be registered again for a line of clothes. But if you were selling a line of boats you could not modify someone's trademark of an anchor and use it yourself.

If a trademark is federally registered in the U.S. Patent and Trademark Office, the ® symbol, or the words "Registered in the U.S. Patent and Trademark Office," must be used. Failure to give this notice prevents you from recovering damages for trademark infringement.

If your trademark or service mark is not registered federally or is registered only in your state, a ™ or SM is used to identify this condition. The ™ or SM symbol must be smaller than the actual trademark and must follow the mark. Before deciding on a size for your ™ symbol, you may wish to look at other marks found on other goods, to get a feel for such things as artwork and the size comparison between the trademark and the symbol.

A trademark is owned by the first person or company to use the mark in commerce, meaning whoever first uses it in public is considered the owner of the mark, whether the mark is registered or not. There are certain conditions which must be met before you can register a trademark. One is that the mark cannot be recorded as belonging to another person or organization. That is why it is advisable when applying for a federal trademark to have a search done, although it is not necessary for state registration.

Another condition is that it must not resemble another mark or be of a content so as to confuse or deceive a buyer. One example of this would be if a trademark said "China Fashions" and the clothes were designed and manufactured in Oklahoma. The trademark would most likely be refused registration.

This should be considered if you intend to start with a state trademark and later obtain a federal trademark; your marketing power could be damaged by having to change your logo midstream. After meeting these conditions, a trademark can be obtained and even licensed. Your trademark is intellectual property, and you have the right to use it and even seek protection from the courts if someone else tries to infringe upon it.

With your trademark also comes a responsibility to maintain adequate quality control. The value of a trademark is that the public sees it as an exclusive sign of a business, and bad news often travels faster than good news.

In cases where the product is sold directly to the consumer, the trademark is extremely valuable. For example, if I knew the formula for Coca-Cola®, and sold it on the market under a different name, many people would say it tasted different, and most Coca-Cola® drinkers would not even try it at all because the consumer has come to rely on certain manufacturers for quality. Once the quality of your product gains a name for itself, others will have the same trouble getting people away from your product to try theirs.

Trademarks should never be underestimated as a marketing tool for product success. Unlike patents, trademarks have an indefinite life when used properly. Federal trademarks are issued for a period of 10 years and can be renewed if still in use.

You can lose a trademark by letting it become generic. This is when people begin using your brand name to describe the type of product, for instance, "Xeroxed" copies instead of photocopies.

A trademark should be used as an adjective modifying a noun. An example of this would be "Scotch® Brand Tape" made by the 3M Company. In calling this same product Scotch Tape, the product becomes generic and the 3M Company could thereby lose its trademark. Terms which were once trademarks but are now public domain include:

Escalator	Linoleum
Lanolin	Corn Flakes
Kerosene	Trampoline

Thermos bottle	Cube Steak
Dry Ice	Mimeograph
Nylon	Raisin Bran
Aspirin	High Octane

All those trademarks were lost because proper precautions were not taken and the names became generic.

Filing a trademark yourself could cost as little as $25 (for a state trademark). Although I've discussed trademarks as they relate to products within the marketplace, there are provisions for reserving a trademark if you are less than six months away from the marketplace.

The Trademark Law Revision Act of 1988, Title 1 of Pub. L. No. 100-667, which went into effect November 16, 1989, allows someone who has a bona fide intent to use the trademark in commerce to apply for federal registration, thus avoiding the need to wait until the trademark is in actual use.

However, the trademark should be used in commerce within six months after the date of issuance of the "Notice of Allowance," and a verified statement of its use should be filed with the Patent and Trademark Office.

Other important provisions of the 1988 Revision Act reduced the registration term from 20 to 10 years. The Act also subjects one who makes a false statement in advertising about one's own or someone else's goods to liability in a civil action brought by any person injured by such statements.

The Federal Trademark Application

A federal trademark application is comprised of:

- A written application form;

- A drawing of the work;

- Three specimens showing actual use of the mark in connection with the goods or service; and

- The required filing fee.

The written application form must be in English and include a heading to identify the mark, a class number, and specify if you are an individual, corporation, or partnership.

To receive the appropriate forms and information to federally register a trademark, write to:

Patent and Trademark Office
Washington DC 20231

Indicate in your letter whether you wish to apply on the basis of actual use or intent to use, and specify whether you're an individual, corporation, or partnership. If you wish to register a trademark in your state, call or write to your secretary of state for forms and instructions. The cost varies from state to state and can range from $10 to $50.

What You Cannot Trademark

These are the types of material which cannot be trademarked:

- Immoral, scandalous, or deceptive matter;
- Trade names;
- Slogans;
- Governmental emblems;
- Personal names;
- Marks which may cause confusion;
- A person's likeness, without that person's consent;
- Geographical locations;
- Descriptive words; and
- Generic words.

Trademarks as Marketing Tools

Can you imagine going to a store and finding products on the shelves without brand names? The inferior products would look exactly the same as the superior products. It wouldn't be long before the better manufacturers lost all incentive to maintain their high quality standards, because they would not enjoy greater sales for their extra efforts.

Trademarks are an important part of our purchasing a product. If you bought a brand-name refrigerator that worked well, you would be more inclined to purchase a stove by the same company, even though they are entirely different products. A company's reputation can make a future product successful simply through its trademark.

Trademark Art

For inventors considering designing their own trademark artwork, you should consult with a graphic artist or industrial designer familiar with trademark design.

A quality trademark will ensure the consumer of a quality product. Your trademark must be well thought out, unique, and, above all, original.

Compulsory Trademark Licensing

By now, you have thought of trademarks which may not follow the established rules. It seems that there are always exceptions to the rules, and one such exception is the trademark "RealLemon®," owned by the Borden Company.

Even though descriptive words cannot be trademarked (see the list of types of material which cannot be trademarked, previous page), occasionally one slips by. In the case of "RealLemon", the Borden Company probably wishes it hadn't slipped past.

After a lengthy legal hearing by a Federal Trade Commission administrative law judge, it was decided that Borden would be required to license its trademarks to all its competitors for a very small royalty. This compulsory license is now available to anyone who asks for it. The end result is a trademark which now has little or no meaning, because the company failed to follow some basic rules.

Copyrights

If your written or artistic endeavor includes any book, poem, speech, recording, computer program, statue, painting, label, cartoon, dramatic or musical work, pantomime, choreographic work, motion picture, video tape, map, game board, packaging design, or instructions, you qualify for a copyright. This book, for example, falls under copyright protection. Copyrights offer legal protection just like patents and trademarks, but are much easier to obtain.

Copyright law in the United States has its foundation in Article I, Section 8, Clause 8, of the Constitution, and is embodied in Title 17 of the United States Code. Under the Federal Copyright Statutes, which were enacted in 1976 and became effective January 1, 1978, there is no longer any state copyright protection.

As the law defines it today, copyrights protect original works of authorship fixed to any tangible medium of expression, including:

Books	Graphics
Drama	Motion pictures
Articles	Sculptured works
Pantomimes	Video recordings
Music	Sound recordings
Choreographic works	Computer software
Pictorials	

The copyright Act grants to authors and artists the exclusive right to reproduce, adapt, revise, and translate as well as distribute, sell, display, and license their works.

Copyright law grants authors, composers, programmers, artists and the like, the right to prevent others from copying, using, or selling their original creation without permission. Copyrights do not give an author rights to the information contained within a book, only the method and style in which the information is presented.

Unlike patents, copyrights are obtained the minute the work assumes some tangible form, and last for 50 years after the creator's death.

Copyright Notice

Under a recent change in copyright law, it is no longer necessary for a copyright notice to be given. Because of this new law, there may be some difficult court cases coming up involving innocent infringers.

Even though it is no longer mandatory, you can still register your work with the copyright office for $10 and give the general public notice of copyright. If you do decide to give notice of copyright on your work, the proper way to do this is to write "Copyright," followed by the year the work is completed, followed by your name or company name. You may also use a © for recordings and records as an alternative to writing "Copyright."

A copyright notice looks something like this:

© **1990 Quest International**

You may also abbreviate "Copyright" to "Copr.," and add the words "All Rights Reserved" below the copyright notice.

To obtain the best information and registration forms, write to the U.S. Copyright Office, Washington, DC 20559 or call (202) 287-9100. There may also be a local phone number to call for copyright information; check your telephone directory.

Because more than half a million copyright applications are received annually, a certificate of registration can take up to 16 weeks to receive.

Copyright Protection

The exclusive rights in copyrighted works are set forth in Title 17, USC §106; these rights, however, are subject to the provisions of 17 USC §§107-108. The exclusive rights listed in Section 106 include:

1. The right to reproduce the copyrighted work in copies or records;

2. The right to prepare derivative works based upon the copyrighted work;

3. The right to distribute copies or records of the copyrighted work to the public, by sale or other transfer of ownership, or by rental, lease, or lending;

4. In the case of literary, musical, dramatic and choerographic works, pantomimes, motion pictures, and other audio-visual works, the right to publicly perform the copyrighted work; and

5. In the case of literary, musical, dramatic, and choreographic works, pantomimes and pictorial, graphic, or cultural works, including the

individual images of a motion picture or other audio-visual work, the right to publicly display the copyrighted work.

Ownership of Copyrights

The ownership of a copyright is initially held by the author or authors of the work. When the copyright is prepared under employment or contract, the employer is the owner. In the same way as with patents and trademarks, the exclusive rights comprising in a copyright may be assigned or licensed. When ownership of a copyright is transferred in any way, the author must inform the copyright office within one month after the execution of the transfer for the transfer to be valid.

An advantage to copyrights is their long life, which can in turn increase the royalty life when licensed.

Trade Secrets

To qualify for a trade secret, you must have information not known by the public which gives you or your company an advantage. Trade secrets include techniques, designs, materials, processes, and formulas.

If you have an idea or information you wish to keep secret, you would qualify for trade secret protection. Trade secrets can be licensed the same way as a patent.

The concept of the trade secret was developed by the judicial system to protect formulas and other manufacturing secrets. In contrast to patents, which usually last 17 years, a trade secret lasts as long as you can keep it a secret. Patents also require a disclosure of the formulas and technologies involved, which can be duplicated. Of course, trade secrets are not as easy to duplicate, due to the fact they are kept secret.

The most famous example of a trade secret is the formula for Coca-Cola®. The basic ingredients are readily identified as water, sugar, caramel coloring, and carbonation; however, the exact quantities and cooking process are masked in mystery and locked away in a high-security vault.

If patented, the formula would be made public, and anyone could send for a copy of the patent, and even try to modify and improve it. The

Coca-Cola® formula will probably remain a trade secret years after an actual patent would have expired.

An idea need not be patentable in order to receive trade secret protection, nor is novelty a requirement. Trade secrets can cover the entire range of business practices.

The Uniform Trade Secrets Act safeguards trade secrets if three conditions are met.

1. The trade secret must have economic value. This can be any proprietary information including formulas, techniques, pricing information, sales forecasts, and customer information which would give another person or company a competitive advantage.

2. Trade secrets must be secret, or unknown to the public and difficult to uncover.

3. The owner of a trade secret must attempt to protect it. If you have employees, they must be made aware of its secrecy. Furthermore, any visiting sales representatives, vendors, customers, inspectors, or the like must be informed of its secrecy if they must access such information. This is usually the hardest requirement in ensuring secrecy.

You might consider a confidentiality or nondisclosure agreement. The best confidentiality or nondisclosure agreements are phrased in a way so as not to define exactly what you consider to be the company's trade secrets.

The definition of your company's proprietary information must be broad enough to cover future advances in technology. The document should contain language strong enough to show a court that you consider your trade secret a vital part of your business and that monetary damages should be in order. Preparing a strong document now could help you avoid a court case later. An additional method of protecting your trade secret is stamping all relevant information "confidential." This can also help courts determine whether or not information was treated as a trade secret. If you feel as though you have competitors who would actually go through your trash, you should consider getting a shredding machine.

Before you go to court to sue a competitor, remember two things: First, a trade secret court case is usually expensive and can take years to resolve. Second, another competitor can sit in on a public hearing and listen to you tell the court your trade secret.

Unfair Competition

Unfair competition is a very broad term defining legal standards of business conduct. It provides protection against such things as simulation of trade packaging, using similar corporate and professional names, misappropriation of trade secrets, and palming off one person's goods as those of another. Many inventors sometimes impressed by a big-name product have a tendency to follow another company's trade dress.

Unfair competition law can be utilized, with or without other forms of protection, to protect your trade dress. For example, if you were selling your unprotected product packaged in a bright-green box with stars on it, and a competitor tried to cash in on your marketing success by using a bright-green box with stars on it, you could stop your competitor by using unfair competition law. The same would apply if a competitor used a similar name, such as changing "Starclips" to "Starclippers." Again using unfair competition law, you could sue any competitor for using similar trade dress.

If your product should too closely resemble another trade dress, you could find an injunction placed against you, prohibiting you from any further activity in the marketplace until a court decides on your guilt or innocence. If found guilty of unfair competition, a judge would award the damaged company compensation in monetary damages for adding to the public's confusion. There are better ways to spend your profits.

Patent Depository Libraries
ALABAMA
Auburn University Library
Auburn University
Auburn, AL 36849
(205) 826-4500

Birmingham Public Library
21 Park Place
Birmingham, AL 35203
(205) 226-3680

ALASKA

Anchorage Municipal Libraries
(907) 264-4481

ARIZONA

Arizona State University Library
Tempe, AZ 85287
(602) 965-7609

ARKANSAS

Arkansas State Library
One Capitol Mall
Little Rock, AR 72201
(501) 371-2090

CALIFORNIA

Los Angeles Public Library
630 West Fifth Street
Los Angeles, CA 90071
(213) 612-3273

California State Library
Library Courts Building
Sacramento, CA 95809
(916) 322-4572

San Diego Public Library
202 C Street
San Diego, CA 92101
(619) 236-5813

University of California General Library
P.O. Box 19557
Irvine, CA 92713
(714) 865-7234

CALIFORNIA (continued)

Patent Information Clearinghouse
Sunnyvale Public Library
665 W. Olive Avenue
Sunnyvale, CA 94086
(408) 730-7290

COLORADO

Denver Public Library
3840 York Street
Denver, CO 80205
(303) 571-2122

CONNECTICUT

Connecticut State Library
231 Capitol Avenue
Hartford, CT 06106
(203) 786-5000

DELAWARE

University of Delaware Library
Newark, DE 19711
(302) 451-2965

FLORIDA

Broward County Main Library
100 South Andrews Avenue
Fort Lauderdale, FL 33301
(305) 357-7444

Miami-Dade Public Library
101 West Flagler Street
Miami, FL 33130
(305) 375-2665

GEORGIA

Georgia Institute of Technology
Price Gilbert Memorial Library
225 North Avenue NW
Atlanta, GA 30332
(404) 894-4508

IDAHO

University of Idaho Library
Moscow, ID 83843
(208) 885-6235

ILLINOIS

Chicago Public Library
400 N. Franklin
Chicago, IL 60602
(312) 269-2865

Illinois State Library
Centennial Building
Springfield, IL 62756
(217) 782-5430

INDIANA

Indianapolis Public Library
40 East St. Clair Street
Indianapolis, IN 46206
(317) 269-1741

LOUISIANA

Louisiana State University – Troy H. Middleton Library
Baton Rouge, LA 70803
(504) 388-2570

MARYLAND

University of Maryland Library
University of Maryland
College Park, MD 20742
(301) 454-3037

MASSACHUSETTS

Boston Public Library
Copley Square
Boston, MA 02117
(617) 536-5400

University of Massachusetts
Amherst, MA 01003
(413) 545-1370

MICHIGAN

University of Michigan – Hatcher Library-South
818 Harlan
Ann Arbor, MI 48109
(313) 764-7494

Detroit Public Library
5201 Woodward Avenue
Detroit, MI 48202
(313) 833-1450

MINNESOTA

Minneapolis Public Library
300 Nicollet Mall
Minneapolis, MN 55401
(612) 372-6570

MISSOURI

Linda Hall Library
5109 Cherry Street
Kansas City, MO 64110
(816) 363-4600

St. Louis Public Library
1301 Olive Street
St. Louis, MO 63103
(314) 241-2288

MONTANA

Montana College of Mineral Science and Technology
Butte, MT 59701
(406) 496-4284

NEBRASKA

University of Nebraska – Lincoln Library
Lincoln, NE 68588
(402) 472-3411

NEVADA

University of Nevada–Reno
Reno, NV 89557
(702) 784-6579

NEW HAMPSHIRE

University of New Hampshire Library
Durham, NH 03824
(603) 862-1777

NEW JERSEY

Newark Public Library
5 Washington Street
Newark, NJ 07101
(201) 733-7815

NEW MEXICO

University of New Mexico General Library
Albuquerque, NM 87131
(505) 277-5441

NEW YORK

New York State Library
Cultural Education Center
Albany, NY 12230
(518) 474-7040

Buffalo and Erie County Public Library
Lafayette Square
Buffalo, NY 14203
(716) 856-7525

The New York Public Library
521 West 43rd Street
New York, NY 10036
(212) 714-8529

NORTH CAROLINA

North Carolina State University – The D.H. Hill Library
Raleigh, NC 27650
(919) 737-3280

OHIO

Public Library of Cincinnati
800 Vine Street
Cincinnati, OH 45202
(513) 369-6936

OHIO (continued)

Cleveland Public Library
325 Superior Avenue
Cleveland, OH 44114
(216) 623-2870

Ohio State University Library
1858 Neil Avenue Mall
Columbus, OH 43210
(614) 422-6286

Toledo Public Library
325 Michigan Street
Toledo, OH 43624
(419) 255-7055

OKLAHOMA

Oklahoma State University Library
Stillwater, OK 74078
(405) 624-6546

OREGON

Portland State University Library
934 SW Harrison
Portland, OR 97207
(503) 378-4239

PENNSYLVANIA

State Library of Pennsylvania
Walnut Street and Commonwealth Avenue
Harrisburg, PA 17105
(215) 686-5330

Carnegie Library of Pittsburgh
4400 Forbes Avenue
Pittsburgh, PA 15217
(412) 622-3138

Pennsylvania State University – Pattee Library
University Park, PA 16802
(814) 865-4861

RHODE ISLAND

Providence Public Library
150 Empire Street
Providence, RI 02903
(401) 521-8726

SOUTH CAROLINA

Medical University of South Carolina
171 Ashley Avenue
Charleston, SC 29425
(803) 792-2371

TENNESSEE

Memphis Public Library
1850 Peabody Avenue
Memphis, TN 38104
(901) 725-8876

Vanderbilt University Library
Nashville, TN 37203
(615) 322-2775

TEXAS

University of Texas at Austin
General Libraries
Austin, TX 78712
(512) 471-1610

Texas A & M University – Sterling C. Evans Library
College Station, TX 77843-5000
(409) 845-2551

Dallas Public Library
1515 Young Street
Dallas, TX 75201
(214) 749-4176

Rice University – The Fondren Library
Houston, TX 77251-1892
(713) 527-8101

UTAH

University of Utah
Salt Lake City 84112
(801) 581-8394

VIRGINIA

Virginia Commonwealth University Library
901 Park Avenue
Richmond, VA 23228
(804) 257-1104

WASHINGTON

University of Washington
Suzzallo Library
Seattle, WA 98195
(206) 543-0740

WISCONSIN

University of Wisconsin
Kurt F. Wendt Engineering Library
215 N. Randall Avenue
Madison, WI 53706
(608) 262-6845

Milwaukee Public Library
814 W. Wisconsin Avenue
Milwaukee, WI 53233
(414) 278-3247

WYOMING

Wyoming State Library
Cheyenne, WY 82002

The address of the main patent library is:

U.S. Patent & Trademark Office Science Library
Crystal Plaza 34
2021 Jefferson Davis Highway
Arlington, VA 22202

NOTES

NOTES

_____

_____

_____

_____

_____

_____

_____

_____

_____

_____

_____

_____

_____

_____

_____

_____

_____

_____

_____

_____

_____

_____

_____

_____

_____

_____

_____

_____

_____

Chapter 3

Prototyping

Turning Ideas Into Reality

An idea is just an idea until it takes some tangible form. In order to add credibility and value to your idea, you must have a prototype.

Prototyping your invention will do more than just prove that the idea works. Prototyping also:

- Tests the materials selection and the manufacturing process you intend to use;
- Generates important data concerning time requirements, processes, and labor; and
- Solves unforeseen problems.

Most important, it will turn that intangible idea into something tangible, a real invention.

Prototyping your invention may be difficult due to the lack of knowledge of processes or difficulty in obtaining materials, but trying to sell an invention without a prototype can be similar to trying to sell the London Bridge without a deed.

Prototyping your invention will lend credibility to your idea, and will also add a perceived value by identifying materials, tooling, fabrication technique, costs, and, in general, your invention's manufacturability. Prototyping is a development stage which also serves as an important evaluation stage.

In developing your prototype you will also discover an evolution as the product becomes more suitable for production. You can expect your invention to change as it becomes more tangible. There may be minor changes such as a material change, for instance, changing from polypropylene to nylon, or an even more apparent change where a design is modified to provide for improved manufacturing.

You need to be flexible and innovative in solving the problems which will become apparent as your idea starts to take shape. Building the prototype is part of being an inventor, so don't worry if you're not an engineer, mechanic, designer, or model maker, because as the inventor you are the one best qualified to build your invention – you see it in your mind and you know what you want. You are the source of the creativity that brought the idea to life. You should also be the one to take it that one step further, into physical being.

Your first prototype may be built of clay, wood, wire, or any usable material. Even the prototype of the car you now drive was made of clay so that the engineers could see any design mistakes and make improvements.

Prototyping will also bring to light problems that may surface in manufacturing your invention, making it easier to solve those problems before actual production starts.

Use the experience of building your prototype to have some fun. Be creative in the ways you might build your invention. I have built prototypes out of some very interesting things which were never meant to do what they wound up doing.

In one situation, an inventor came to me with a very good idea, but it was too expensive for the market, due to a remote control device needed for its operation. By looking, not at industry to supply the remote control, but a toy store, I was able to reduce the part's cost from about $200 to about $3. In prototyping, it pays to look around and mix industries.

Spend as much time as possible browsing through the aisles of different stores. By doing so, you will discover that parts you find in one industry sometimes work in other industries. I try to catalog my unusual finds for later use; you never know when this kind of research will pay off.

Once, while working on a Small Business Innovation Research (SBIR) project through the Air Force, I needed an inexpensive fire sprinkler nozzle for chemical dispersal. While the fire protection industry had the nozzles I needed, they cost $20 to $30. Because of my past research of other industries, I remembered plastic irrigation nozzles at the garden supply store which would do basically the same thing, and sold for 30 cents each. Not only did I save money and provide better marketing potential, soon after I developed a plastic nozzle for the fire protection industry. Now I wonder where that idea came from.

Sometimes a prototype will need to be redesigned in order to utilize existing or readily available parts, so don't be discouraged if you find yourself going back to the drawing board many times. That's a very important part of the prototyping experience and it will often improve your invention.

Using Efficient Designs

Prototypes usually have one thing in common: They can be expensive to build and rarely lend themselves to mass production.

Although your first prototype is usually dedicated to making your invention workable, you should note any improvements which will help you develop a more efficient design. The prototype stage is important in fine tuning your invention by developing the best possible design at an early stage.

Prototyping your invention should serve as an evaluation process in developing a more efficient design. By efficient design, I mean discovering labor-saving steps, removing or redesigning parts difficult to assemble, and basically streamlining the process of building your invention. With these improvements, your invention becomes more suitable to manufacturing and marketing, and becomes more valuable in contract negotiating as well. Removing unnecessary processes or steps early on reduces the cost, which later will add to your profits and sales success.

Last year I attended a national workshop on design for manufacturing and assembly, dealing with design efficiency. I remember thinking on my flight to Rhode Island, where the workshop was to be held, that this was probably going to be a waste of time. I have always taken pride in having a lot of common sense and can usually view a problem from many different perspectives. So I didn't really think I was going to learn anything new. As it turned out, I did learn something. I learned even common sense can be repackaged.

All too often we do not take the proper approaches to even the simplest problems. Many inventors suffer from the "I-can't-see-the-forest-for-the-trees" syndrome. There are so many methods for solving a problem, and the method is never as important as the solution. Inventors especially have a tendency to become protective about their ideas. The same determination which helps us become inventors will at times hinder us in finding solutions to getting our invention to market.

To demonstrate the importance of looking at a problem from a different angle, let's look at some of the companies using design-efficiency programs today:

NCR Corporation recently produced a cash register terminal which had 15 parts and could be snapped together in less than two minutes by someone wearing a blindfold. This new terminal reduced assembly time by 75% and reduced the number of parts by 80%, compared to their old unit. Fewer parts and less assembly time also reduced testing and packaging, resulting in an estimated $1.1 million savings because of reduced manufacturing costs.

IBM Corporation redesigned its Proprinter® several years ago; it can now be assembled in only three minutes with 79% fewer parts than its predecessor. Ford used more efficient manufacturing and assembly methods when redesigning the new Taurus, and achieved estimated savings of $1 billion.

Optimum Design for Manufacturing and Assembly

Entering the world of manufacturing and marketing has always had its hurdles, but the 1990s will require even more expertise and knowledge to overcome these hurdles because of emerging new and advanced technologies.

Because of the new Europe, advancing Far Eastern countries, and the newly liberated Eastern Bloc countries, all importing more of their technologies to U.S. markets every day, the United States now has to compete with world-class quality products from around the world, as well as here in the states.

Due to the unbalanced trade deficit and the fact that many U.S. firms are trailing far behind the Japanese and other countries in both product expertise and technology, it's even more important to understand the many new methodologies and processes being developed, to assist U.S. firms in becoming competitive again.

Regaining the Competitive Edge

According to a report given to the House of Representatives on October 19, 1988, by the Congressional Committee on Science, Space, and Technology, the United States is losing more than $340 million a day in trade to foreign competitors. The report stated that if trade is to be brought back into balance, Americans will have to produce more products at home and will have to sell more here and abroad. U.S. firms, said the report, are not able to take technology and use it to produce high-quality products in the short time periods that Japanese firms can.

The report further stated that the greatest challenge with respect to America's international competitiveness lies in the education and training of its people. Particular emphasis is needed on technical expertise directly related to product and manufacturing processes.

The International Trade Administration, Office of Trade and Analysis, U.S. Department of Commerce estimates that more than $119 billion worth of imports come into the U.S. each year.

In the United States, good design involves more than a drawing by which to assemble parts. Product design, or industrial design, involves much more than simply building a product. Today's inventor or industrial designer must take into account such matters as product liability risk, feasibility studies, model making, and accelerated life testing.

Today, product designers must implement cost reductions by the simplification of a design and determine methods of measuring how efficient a design is, in terms of assembly. It has long been recognized that by reducing the number of parts within a design, you will benefit from several advantages, one of which is reduced cost. Fewer parts also adds to the quality of a product by removing possible weak links and thereby decreasing maintenance problems; the remaining parts must then be easy to manufacture and assemble.

Because inventors usually build prototypes early in the development of their product, their consideration is generally based on getting the idea or product to work. Most products are never really designed for considerations of manufacturing.

Industry has learned that a formalized step-by-step process to analyze a product promotes better design. Given this systematic approach to design, the inventor or designer of a new product can evaluate and analyze, within its design stages, a competitive product.

Studies within the area of design have determined that as much as 85% of the cost can be designed out of a product, while still in the design stage. The inventor, as a product designer, must be aware of the nature of the different assembly processes and must understand why one process may be more efficient than another. If you are unable to give a sound reason for using a certain process, you may not be as familiar with the suggested process as you need to be and may be unaware of other, more efficient processes which could reduce cost and improve quality.

A product designer must have a sound reason for requiring separate parts which increase assembly time and material cost. Ask yourself if several parts can be combined into one manufactured item. Any combination of parts will eliminate at least one operation in assembly; the combination of parts will further enhance quality, performance, and maintenance.

Some companies use a producibility engineering methodology which dictates that an engineer avoid complicated or difficult features, but the outcome can often be a large number of simple parts with a high assembly cost and poor reliability. This may be a reasonable alternative only if assembly labor costs are extremely low.

In many cases, the product designer has no knowledge of machine operation cost, process cost, how the design affects assembly, and why many processes are used. An example of this is today's automobile, which can have as many as 20 different kinds of plastics and dozens of different fastener types, all requiring separate tools.

Optimum Design Process

Optimum design can be many things to the people working within different areas of production, some of which include:

- A method for evaluating and reducing manufacturing cost of a product during conceptual stages of product development;

- A method of obtaining more efficient assembly procedures;

- A method of anticipating future problems in manufacturing;

- Simultaneous or concurrent engineering;

- A method to improve quality by making the product simpler;

- A communication tool (communications with manufacturing to understand problems and adjust accordingly);

- A procedure that considers production factors at the design stage.

Importance of Optimum Design

There are several good reasons for using optimum design as the means for considering factors and variables.

1. Optimum design improves product cost, reliability, productivity, and competitiveness. It also reduces inventory and paper work.

2. After manufacturing starts on a product, there are substantial costs for improvements.

3. Research shows that 70% to 80% of a product's cost is determined in the first 5% of its design life.

4. Once the initial design is set, few people go back and develop a totally new concept; most changes are merely modifications.

5. In many products, fasteners outnumber functional parts, representing a major portion of assembly time.

6. Designing for productivity saves dollars which can be utilized toward marketing success.

7. A screw may be an easy way to hold two assemblies together, but a snap-fit can eliminate screws and reduce assembly cost.

By using the best design, overhead costs relating to the product are reduced. Some of the contributing factors related to design include cost accounting, direct labor administration, equipment depreciation, insurance, energy, engineering changes, production maintenance, material handling, quality control, inspection, purchasing, receiving, planning, documentation, inventory, and distribution.

Optimum design will assist in the development of a quality product by allowing for fewer processing steps, fewer adjustments, fewer mating parts, fewer tolerance stack-up problems, fewer operator frustrations, fewer material control problems, and fewer assembly fixtures.

Rules for Optimum Design

1. **Reduce the number of parts.** Eliminating parts or reducing the number of different types of parts can have many different benefits, including decreased material, assembly, and tool costs; improved product quality; reduction in overhead costs because of less documentation, small inventories, fewer suppliers, simplified production control, fewer inspections, less rework, and so on.

2. **Strive to eliminate adjustments.** Parts should be designed so that mating surfaces fall into place easily. This can be accomplished by using tapers, chamfers, aligning features, etc. Part functions should be incorporated; functions should be moved closer together to facilitate less linkage and reduce the need for adjustments; and when possible, electronic correction should be used as a substitute for mechanical alignment. Alignment features can be costly, but the added cost is usually offset by a reduction in assembly time. Parts which are not self-securing should be located immediately on assembly. Avoid the need for clamps. Ensure that parts are located before they are released. Use pilot point screws to avoid cross-threading problems.

3. **Consider access and visibility for each operation.** Restricted vision and access can make a simple operation a difficult one; always consider clearance for hands and tools. Parts that ordinarily are easy to assemble can have difficulties due to handling or separating them in bulk. To avoid handling difficulties, include features to prevent

nesting (intertwining or locking together). To ensure nontangling, always specify closed-end or compression coil springs. Include safe holding features for parts with sharp edges. Avoid parts such as E-clips and snap rings which require special tools.

4. **Design parts to be easily installed.** Eliminate situations where a part can be installed incorrectly. Provide some type of obstruction that will prohibit incorrect assembly and make parts symmetrical so that assembly orientation is not difficult. Use arrows or matching lines for quick alignment of parts which require orientation.

5. **Maximize part symmetry.** The more symmetrical a part is, the quicker it can be oriented during the handling phase of assembly. Parts to avoid are those with only a slight asymmetry. If the functional features cannot be made clearly asymmetrical, a clearly visible nonfunctional feature should be added to define the orientation.

To test your product for optimum design, consider these guidelines.

■ Test the need for each part's existence as a separate part. Is there a requirement during assembly or operation which demands separate materials or movement?

■ Use integral locking features, such as captured washers to reduce assembly time.

■ Move the functional components into proximity with one another to reduce connecting cables, linkages, wires, etc.

■ Use multifunctional parts if possible.

■ Use off-the-shelf items only when they meet your requirements exactly.

Production Planning

Production planning may be a term you have heard in industry and felt only affected planners in large companies making sure materials, resources, assembly labor, and equipment were ready as needed.

The fact is, smaller companies require planned production even more than larger companies, due to the vulnerability of smaller operations relying on sole-source suppliers. If your product depends on a certain part and that part becomes unavailable, what are your options?

Many times you will have to speculate on production needs. Your marketing plan will, of course, help in these matters, but consumer response will ultimately be the deciding factor.

Many new ventures use manual labor, based upon the assumption that it is the least expensive form of labor, although in some cases this is not true. Poor production and not being able to respond to the demand of an increasing market can cost you both sales and profits.

Taking into account production volume, number of parts within the assembly and most methods of assembly, the designer may discover robot or special-purpose transfer assembly machines are best suited from the beginning.

If you're in a situation where you feel limited production will soon become high production, high-speed automatic assembly would be a better investment in product competitiveness, even with amortization and higher product cost at first. Your situation may even require contract or private-label assembly until volumes reach the appropriate or desired level.

Deciding the magic number in production requires an understanding of payback schedules and cost data. Finding the proper volumes for payback of automatic assembly, however, can make the difference in whether your product can remain competitive as volumes increase.

Analysis Procedures

To analyze your design and identify features resulting in high assembly costs, follow these steps:

Step 1. Obtain the best information about the product or assembly. Useful items include engineering drawings, exploded three-dimensional views, an existing version of the product, or a prototype.

Step 2. Take the assembly apart (or imagine how this might be done).

Step 3. Reassemble the product one piece at a time, looking for problem areas.

If you have sufficient information to consider high production, become familiar with the high-speed or robotic tools available for your industry and include these considerations within the analysis.

In your analysis, consider whether parts are added one at a time during assembly. This would be the case for some assembly lines where workers add only one part at each station. However, for bench assembly and on many other assembly lines, the workers will often handle two parts simultaneously. Consider if the parts are presented in bulk and randomly oriented, or available in magazines or special containers.

Performing this analysis provides useful information which can result in a reduction in parts and assembly time.

Designing for High-Speed and Robot Assembly

The most important and difficult consideration, for high-speed automatic assembly or robot assembly, is the efficiency with which the individual parts can be handled automatically.

The basis for cost comparisons will in many cases require expert redesign, yet for the production which warrants such changes, the cost savings will be considerable.

Here are some general rules to be applied in high-speed automatic assembly:

1. Ensure that parts can be easily separated from bulk and conveyed along the track of a vibratory or hopper feeder.

2. Avoid parts which tangle, are flexible, have thin or tapered edges which can overlap, are fragile, sticky, or oily.

3. Use parts which are easily oriented, such as symmetrical parts or those with projections, notches, or other orienting features.

Because of the expert nature of the design requirements for automatic assembly, you will need to become knowledgeable in such design features or consult with experts in the field.

Considering Product Liability

Privity is a legal term meaning a direct relationship between two parties. When products of the past failed, causing harm, manufacturers argued that the product was distributed by a wholesaler or retailer and privity was absent.

In one landmark case, *MacPherson v. Buick Motor Co.*, the plaintiff was driving a new car when one of its wheels fell off, resulting in injury. Buick declared that the defective axle came from another manufacturer and therefore it had no liability.

The judge, however, ruled that Buick was liable because of its responsibility to remove danger from the car. The newness of the car eliminated negligence in maintenance of the owner. The product must not only be safe while in use, but also during distribution and retirement (discarding). Potential product liability risk can be designed out of a product by following certain guidelines, including:

- Design to nationally recognized standards;

- Use components with statistical reliability;

- An accelerated aging test can be valuable in discovering defects and disputing testimony of design defect in product liability suits;

- Make a worst case analysis of the product;

- Drawings must have notes to manufacturing to eliminate hazards, e.g., remove burrs, plating notes, etc. A drawing without notes determining a quality standard can lose a liability suit;

- Record product development history and design decision reasoning;

- Consider shipping vibration, which can weaken parts not designed for abnormal fatigue;

- Use warning labels where appropriate;

- Include proper instructions for use; and

- Use independent testing whenever possible.

Warranties

Warranties must also be considered when thinking about liability. There are two kinds of warranties: express and implied.

Express warranties are defined by the Uniform Commercial Code to be: Any promise made by the seller that influenced the sale; and any description that influenced the sale, e.g., pictures, ads, brochures, etc.

Implied warranties communicate that, because the product is for sale, the manufacturer has made every effort to make sure the product is safe and has at least the minimum qualities expected.

In 1975, Congress passed the Magnuson-Moss Warranty Act, in an attempt to clarify the extent of any warranty given by a manufacturer. This led to the limited warranty, which limits compensation to the buyer.

If you are in the development stages when design may be changed in light of possible faults, obviously the time and efforts are well worth it. The responsibility of the design lies with the inventor as well as with the professional engineer.

Product Life Cycles

There are four life cycle stages of a product:

Production — From raw material to usable product.

Distribution — Transfer of the product to the consumer.

Consumption — The use of the product by the customer.

Retirement — The disposal of the product.

Each of these stages requires consideration during the design of a new product. The production of raw materials can present liabilities to the production or assembly worker which must be addressed. Even distribution carries liability; if your product is improperly packaged and causes liability, you are responsible. One such case involved a longshoreman who fell through a void in a large cardboard package. Even though the man was walking on the packaging, the courts felt the distributor should have been prepared for such events.

Standards

Designing to established standards can be your best protection for reducing your product liability risk. the *Product Standards Index*, second edition, by V. L. Roberts, published by Pergamon Press, identifies many standard-writing organizations and lists standards that apply to various products.

Some important organizations to be considered as sources are:

American National Standards Institute (ANSI) is the main clearinghouse for standards.

Underwriters Laboratories (U.L.) is perhaps best known for the U. L. label, which is applied to products that pass rigorous testing, using one or more of its 350 standards. The U. L. label is well-recognized as evidence of satisfactory design.

American Society for Testing and Materials (ASTM) publishes more than 4,000 standards which identify test procedures and test equipment.

National Fire Protection Association (NFPA) publishes all standards related to fire protection equipment. The National Electrical Code (NEC) is published under NFPA standards.

National Safety Council (NSC) devotes its efforts to accident prevention.

Food and Drug Administration (FDA) originated with the Food and Drug Act of 1906. Among many other products, cosmetics must conform to FDA standards.

Federal Trade Commission (FTC) warns the public when a product is unsafe. Among its other actions, the FTC was involved in the removal of a certain type of imported doll from the market when it was found that the doll's eyes were actually poisonous seeds.

Other organizations dealing with standards include the Occupational Safety and Health Administration (OSHA), the Consumer Product Safety Commission, and the Environmental Protection Agency (EPA).

Groups involved in consumer products include Consumer Research of Washington, New Jersey, and Consumer Reports of Orangeburg, New York.

Considerations of Form and Function

Much of what has been covered so far in this chapter falls within the realm of Industrial Design. Industrial designers are basically professional inventors who conceive ideas, build prototypes, research, and develop new products.

Industrial design came into being more than 50 years ago, because of a public that demanded convenience in every aspect of their lives. They also demanded that convenience be attractive – new products had to not only look as though they were capable of doing their job; they also had to enhance the looks of the home or office. The industrial designer, therefore, had to be concerned with the form, color, and texture of a product, as well as its functionality.

These considerations are still very important today. Consumers many times still think of plastics as being inexpensive, glass as being breakable, aluminum or stainless steel as being long lasting, steel as being strong, fine grained wood as being expensive, and leather or silk as being elegant. Even texture and color affect a product's appeal.

The mechanics of a product may require engineering and science, but designing the appearance is pure art.

Finding Needed Materials

In building your first prototype you will most likely purchase your needed material at the local hardware store or have it made at the local machine shop. Later, you will need to find industrial suppliers for larger quantities and also to avoid paying retail price. Part of the prototyping process is finding future suppliers. Another benefit in dealing directly with the manufacturer is free samples. When was the last time a retail store offered you that?

The best source for obtaining information on where to locate appropriate manufacturers is your city or county library, usually in the business and technology department.

Manufacturers directories available for your use include the *Thomas Register*, *U.S. Industrial Directory*, and *MacRae's Blue Book*.

The *Thomas Register* is a good starting point. It consists of several volumes that list nearly everything under the sun, such as a company's address, phone numbers, product lines, and net sales per year. There are additional sections which include company catalogs and company profiles as well. Not only will the *Thomas Register* help you find materials, it will also help you find potential licensees and competitors.

The *U.S. Industrial Directory* and *MacRae's Blue Book* also work well as additional research sources. All three sources should be used because some companies will only be listed in one of the three directories.

In addition to these directories, the public library also has numerous directories for specific regions and industries. Many libraries now have these catalogs and directories on computer databases for keyword searching.

Some other sources for finding prototyping materials include:

Hexcel Corporation
P.O. Box 2197
20701 Nordhoff Street
Chatsworth, CA 91311
A good source of epoxy and urethane resins for model makers and prototypes.

Merrell Scientific
1965 Buffalo Road
Rochester NY 14626
A source for science equipment and chemicals.

Obtaining Assistance

When building your prototype you may find you need assistance in developing the materials required for your invention.

Most companies have employees whose job it is to solve the problems of potential or existing customers. As a potential customer interested in doing business with a company, you have access to the company's engineers, designers and sales people. Their job is to assist you, even though a customer may use only a portion of the available services.

The most effective way to obtain these and other services is to be sincere in dealing with a company and act professionally. You can reap benefits from using company experts; you may be their biggest customer some day.

Other than obtaining parts and materials for your prototype, you may find that you need someone to actually build the prototype. Finding professional help in this area can sometimes be difficult because such people are not always listed in the Yellow Pages under prototype builders. The best way to find a professional who could build your invention is to look for local manufacturers who work in related fields or look for industrial model builders.

Another good method for obtaining prototyping assistance is to check out local schools, colleges, vocational/technical programs, and universities. Many of these schools require class projects and student assignments each year. This process of prototype building can produce a quality product which will be very inexpensive. On the down side, it may take several months to complete. Remember, you have one year from completion of a working model of your invention to file a patent application.

One important point to keep in mind when using the services of others is that an unpaid prototype builder could become a legal partner in your invention. A good practice when having other people work on your invention is to have them sign a nondisclosure agreement and to get a receipt for your file for all paid work they do. An ounce of prevention initially can eliminate an unwanted partner later.

Tips for Building Your Own Prototype

Building your own prototype is probably one of the best aspects of inventing. You are the one uniquely qualified to develop your idea into a tangible product, and with a few tips, you may find that it's not as hard as you thought it would be.

One important aspect about building prototypes is attitude. Be creative, have fun, and try as many variations as possible with the invention. No professional could possibly share the excitement and enthusiasm you will feel when building your own prototype.

Don't let industrial processes intimidate you. The libraries are full of how-to books on most every process known. Injection molding was once done with hydraulic jacks and plastic cooked in pots. Vacuum forming can be done at home using your stove, vacuum cleaner, and plaster of Paris. Molds for pouring lead, rubber, and plastic can be made out of auto-body putty. The tools exist to do almost anything if you're willing to seek them out.

I recently made a set of molds by using silicone adhesive. Using silicone to form around a part can offer you a mold for limited production. Since silicone can be bought at the hardware store for about $2 a tube, it can be very inexpensive prototype tooling. Charcoal lighter fluid will thin most silicones, which can then be applied by brush. Going to the library and reading different formula books will give you other ideas as well.

One excellent book is *Ingenious Mechanisms For Designers and Inventors*, published by Industrial Press Inc., 200 Madison Ave., New York, New York. Additional books for use in mechanical design are, *507 Mechanical Movements* and *998 Curious Mechanical Movements*. Both books are available through Lindsay Publications Inc., P.O. Box 12, Bradley, Illinois, 60915-0012, or call (815) 468-3668.

Processes

Many times inventors are not knowledgeable on all the processes which exist in industry. The list below will help familiarize you with some processes available.

Blow Molding — A hollow extruded plastic tube is positioned so mold cavities close while air is forced into the tube, forcing plastic to take the shape of the mold. The blow molding process is used in making, among other things, two-liter soda bottles.

Electric Discharge Machining (EDM) — Machine operation which employs direct electrical current to "arc" away metal.

Extrusion Molding — Continuous formation of tubes, pipes, and shapes of metal, plastic, and other suitable materials through the use of forming dies.

Hobbing — A ductile metal billet is placed within a hardened retainer ring to be plunged into a formed cavity.

Injection Molding — The process of extruding molten material into mold cavities, allowing the hot material to form and cool. Normally used with plastic and powdered metals.

Investment Casting — A metal casting process. A wax model of the part is prepared and imbedded in a special slurry of refractory. After the slurry has been poured, it is vacuumed to remove air bubbles. When the refractory has set up and dried, it is placed in a high temperature oven and the material becomes fired, melting the wax and leaving a hollow void. Thereafter, molten metal is poured into the cavity remaining, sometimes by spin casting.

Lay-up — Plastic manufacturing process involving the use of an original pattern upon which a fiber cloth or mat like fiberglass, burlap, or sisal is combined with catalyzed polyester or epoxy liquid resin to form a hardened shape.

Machining — Employing milling machines, either vertical or horizontal, which cut away metal, drill holes, or slot and shape, tap threads, and otherwise sculpt solid material such as metal, plastic, or wood.

Rotational Molding — A process for making hollow parts, using a prepolymerized liquid plastic resin.

Sand Casting — A metal-forming process. A cavity is formed by pressing a pattern into a bed of sand. Molten metal is poured into the cavity and cools to harden. Generally employed for rougher and sturdier parts such as manhole covers, machinery bases, and the like.

Spin Casting — A metal casting process in which molten metal is centrifuged into the mold cavities, rather than poured in, Used in making high-finish and accuracy parts.

Thermoforming/Vacuum forming — A sheet of plastic is heated and drawn or pressured down over a pattern to create a finished shape. Used for making covers and formed shapes. Plastics which can be thermoformed are acrylics, nylon, polyethylene, polystyrene or styrene, polyfluorocarbons, vinyls, polyvinylidene, ABS, acetal resin, polypropylene and polycarbonates.

Transfer Molding — Used for thermosetting plastics. The plastic is cured in a mold under heat and pressure. Usually used to facilitate the molding of intricate products with small, deep holes or numerous metal inserts.

Solvent Molding — Based on the fact that when a mold is immersed in a solution and withdrawn, or when it is filled with a liquid plastic and then emptied, a layer of plastic film adheres to the sides of the mold. Used for products like bathing caps.

High Pressure Laminating — Uses high heat and pressures to hold plastic to reinforcing materials that comprise the body of the finished product. Used for formed shapes which need reinforcing.

Die Casting — Inexpensive, fast, and accurate, but can only use nonferrous alloys because of their low melting temperatures.

Do-It-Yourself Shops

A favorite hangout of mine used to be a local do-it-yourself shop. It served me well for nearly anything I ever needed done regarding prototyping. Unfortunately, this shop, although very popular, is no longer in business. There are, however other similar operations that provide a complete woodworking and machine shop for a monthly fee. These types of clubs can often be found in the Yellow Pages under "Woodworking" or "Hobby Clubs."

Do-it-yourself shops not only provide you with the resources to build your prototype, but they also expose you to many other skilled people who use the facilities. Most of these shops are inexpensive to join and offer expert help to inventors, a lucky find for any inventor.

Many inventors use these facilities to begin production before committing to production facilities. The "co-op" environment is also a plus for inventors seeking assistance.

On visits to the local do-it-yourself shop, I've discovered members using new materials with which I was not familiar. To become more educated I, from time to time, looked over a few shoulders and usually learned something new to use in my prototyping. Likewise, I'm always happy to stop and explain a new process to other inventors.

The Inventors' Workshop

An inventors' workshop can be important to the prototyping of your invention. Your workshop may be the kitchen table, basement, or garage, or it may even be your whole house or apartment. Having a place to work and think is important because of the inspiration and attitude a special place can offer. Try putting an executive on a street corner to make that next big deal, and you'll understand the importance of environment.

An ideal work space will have a drawing board for sketching or drawing plans, a library of resource materials, and, of course, a work area for building that idea. Inventors' workshops are usually cluttered with scrap parts, hardware, and other odds and ends.

I've found that most inventors rarely throw anything away. My workshop includes at least 20 years of accumulated gadgets, broken appliances, and whatchamacallits, which I treasure like the rare collection it truly is.

Why go buy or build something when you already have something almost like it in the garage? To an inventor, that old toaster is just the part for that new neutron heater. Sometimes, just looking at my gadgets will help me create something new.

Mold-Making Materials for Inventors

Materials which inventors should keep around their workshops include these:

Plaster of Paris — Also known as casting plaster, it is inexpensive, readily available, has no odor, and is quick setting. It's easy to mix and is also good for reinforcing flexible molds such as latex. Plaster of Paris is good for both large and small molds and will last longer if you seal it with a lacquer or varnish. A good release agent for molds is polyvinyl alcohol, zinc stearate, or silicone spray. Materials suitable for using with plaster of Paris include polyester and epoxy resins, fiberglass, plaster, concrete, and urethane foam. When preparing a mold for fiberglass, seal the plaster of Paris with three or four coats of thinned shellac.

Latex — is easy to clean, water soluble, non-toxic, non-flammable, and good for up to 50 copies. Latex is very flexible and must be brushed on in thin layers. Latex is better for smaller- to moderate-sized models of wood, ceramics, plaster, cement, water-based clay, synthetic and oil-based clay, brass, bronze, copper, glass, wax, and plastics. The best release agents are silicone spray, liquid wax, and polyvinyl alcohol. The best materials for casting in latex are urethane rubber, cpoxy, polyester resins, fiberglass, plaster, cement, and concrete.

Room temperature vulcanizing rubber — also known as RTV silicone and silicone sealer, can be used up to 100 times for molds. Cures at room temperature. It is nontoxic, flexible, durable, and has a good temperature resistance for casting wax and metals with low melting points. It needs 24 hours for curing and is good for small- to medium-sized models. Models can be metal, ceramic, concrete, plaster, wood, wax, or glass. Release agents are not needed for most materials, although for ceramics a petroleum jelly thinned with paint thinner works well. Materials best used for casting include candle wax, urethane foam, plaster, concrete, polyester resins, and metals with low melting points.

Rigid urethane — also known as Trymer 9501 and rigid foam insulation, is an interesting material used for forming your own molds. It is easy to carve and shape and can be used to run vacuum-formed parts directly from mold. The material is inexpensive and is used to make very large molds. I have used rigid urethane to make parts as large as ten feet long and three feet high.

Prototype Evolution

Remember, the prototype phase of inventing is also an evaluation phase; an evolution takes place as your idea begins to take shape and gain that finished production look.

As your product develops throughout the prototyping phase, take time to step back, evaluate, and study your creation. This is the most important stage in the product's development and a time to put your dreams to the test. If your invention can survive the prototyping process, it will have a far better chance of surviving the manufacturing and marketing stages. The success of your invention starts when you turn your idea into something tangible.

Tax Write-Offs

Depending upon your situation, you may be entitled to certain tax benefits. You should therefore keep all receipts for your prototype development. However, due to the complexity of tax laws and the many factors which must be considered in determining whether your expenses are deductible, you should contact your tax planner for advice.

21st Century Prototyping

For those of you who can afford to go all out on prototyping, there are two prototyping processes which can also be relatively inexpensive to use for the small business. The first is stereolithography and the second is metal-spray moldmaking. The processes work well together.

Stereolithography, a process developed by 3D Systems, Inc., in Valencia, California, combines computer-aided design (CAD) with photocuring to build three-dimensional parts. The operation employs photocurable polymers that change from liquid to solid in the presence of ultraviolet light. A helium-cadmium scanning laser, similar to those in CD players, supplies the radiation. A stainless steel vat that contains the photopolymer, and a "slice" computer, make up the rest of the stereolithography apparatus (SLA).

First, CAD software converts the solid or surface data to a faceted triangle format. SLA software then "slices" the three-dimensional model into a series of two-dimensional cross sections, and defines each section's boundaries. It then fills the boundaries with structural cross hatching and constructs the top and bottom skins using a series of tightly spaced surface vectors. Controlled by computer-generated vector patterns, X-Y galvanometer mirrors direct the beam along the photopolymer's surface. As the mirrors translate, the beam cures and hardens the plastic. The operator, meanwhile, can watch each section's development on the slice computer's monitor.

Although the process sounds like it still belongs in the future, the reality of the process shows just how one invention can assist in the building of another.

Once the stereolithography is complete, the moldmaking process begins by spraying the plastic model with an atomized stream of molten metal. The metal, a Kirksite alloy developed by TAFA Inc., of Concord, New Hampshire, feeds into an arc spray gun as two electrically charged wires which intersect at the gun's head create a high-temperature arc. While the arc melts the feedstock, a 50 cubic foot per minute (cfm) jet of air blows the molten metal against the master. The particles interlock and solidify upon impact to form a dense, hard shell.

The molten particles of metal, because they are surrounded by the high-velocity air stream, do not damage the plastic master. The shell's temperature, in fact, never exceeds 150 degrees.

Once removed from the master, the mold is placed in the cavity of a pre-machined aluminum block and backed up with an epoxy binder. The shell and block form the die at one-third the cost of the traditional tooling process. Lead time is also cut to about one-third. Although this method may not work for all applications, its success is growing fast and will soon spin off other improved methods.

Although building your own prototype is recommended, there are times when it just can't be done. In this case the following list will help you locate a prototype builder near you.

Prototype Builders

Bond's Custom Manufacturing, Inc.
12555 W. 52nd Avenue
Arvada, CO 80002

Central Machine Products, Inc.
2709-B NE 20th Way
Gainsville, FL 32609

Model Builders, Inc.
6155 S. Oak Park Avenue
Chicago, IL 60638

Precision Enterprise, Inc.
999 Main Street, Suite 203-A
Glen Ellyn, IL 60137

New Castle Engineering, Inc.
555 North 12th Street
New Castle, IN 47362

Doerfer Engineering
Department M
201 Washington Street
Cedar Falls, IA 50613

Lion Tool & Die Company, Inc.
607 Marigny Street
New Orleans, LA 70117

Pan-Tec, Inc.
12 Republic Road
Billerica, MA 01821

Versatile Manufacturing Company
8061 Marsh Road
Algonac, MI 48001

Modern Engineering Services Company
28150 Dequindre Road
Warren, MI 48092

Mid-City Precision, Inc.
7430 Oxford Street
Minneapolis, MN 55426

Micro Precision, Inc.
P.O. Box 815
Sunapee, NH 03782

Joule, Inc.
1245 Route 1 South
Edison, NJ 08818

Production Previews, Inc.
29 E. 21st Street
New York, NY 10010

Belcan Engineering Corporation
10200 Anderson Way
Cincinnati, OH 45242

GDA Technical Models
255 Industrial Drive
Franklin, OH 45005

Berks Engineering Company
6th & Chestnut
Reading, PA 19611

Bel Air Tool Corporation
111 Byfield Street
Warwick, RI 02888

Smoak Manufacturing Co.,Inc.
Department M
P.O. Box 749
Orangeburg, SC 29116

Applied Engineering, Inc.
1900 E. Highway 50
Yankton, SD 57078

Design & Production, Inc.
7110 Rainwater Road
Lorton, VA 22079

Medalist Steel Products
2400 W. Cornell
Milwaukee, WI 53209

If you want to test your prototype for safety reasons, call the American Council of Independent Laboratories in Washington, D.C., to locate a testing laboratory near you. The phone number is (202) 877-5872.

Other sources are:

Directory of Testing Laboratories
American Society for Testing and Materials
1916 Race Street
Philadelphia, PA 19103

Directory of the American Council of Independent Laboratories
1725 K Street, NW
Washington, DC 20006

NOTES

NOTES

Chapter 4

Researching

When people think of an inventor, they conjure up images of an absent-minded, wild-haired professor, working in a laboratory filled with bubbling test tubes and elaborate electronic machines, or at a blackboard filled with intricate mathematical calculations. To many people, an inventor is a strange combination of scientist and dreamer, but people rarely consider him an expert. In fact, most inventors really are experts in their own fields.

Researching your invention is a sound investment which will affect every stage of your product development. Just as a patent search will inform you of your chances for gaining a patent, the general research you do will assist you in the development and marketing of your product.

Research can assist you in finding similar products or parts to make your product. It can teach you new processes or even where to market. In short, there is very little that researching can't help you with.

Research may not seem all that thrilling at times, but it's an important way of strengthening your armor when being questioned by a potential licensee. When it comes time to license or market your invention, any lack of knowledge will become apparent. A little research now can help you avoid saying "I don't know," later.

Consider time spent at the library as an investment in your invention. The mere thought of paying a researcher $25 to $50 an hour can make that easy to swallow.

In general, the library is always the best first stop when doing any kind of research. All libraries offer great riches if you remember some of the basic guidelines:

- Remember that libraries work in systems. No library has everything, but collectively, there are endless possibilities.

- Don't judge a library by its size. All libraries have something to offer, including the services of the librarian.

- Remember that when working with librarians, your right to confidentiality is assured.

- Libraries offer professional guidance and will assist you in a variety of search strategies.

- Take the time to browse, especially in the reference sections.

Why Research?

Information will help the inventor compete. Without it, your potential is limited. One inventor recently asked me for information on how to sell some jewelry she had invented. I consulted the Directory of Conventions and referred her to a list of jewelry trade shows that are held throughout the United States. I suggested she look in the library phone books for other wholesalers in such areas as Los Angeles and New York. Not having this information was holding her back; a little research opened the gates to success. If your invention fails for lack of information, you have no one to blame but yourself.

An interesting fact of library-user studies shows that between 10% and 20% of adults account for 90% to 95% of all books borrowed from U.S. libraries. This could explain why so many new businesses fail.

Academic Libraries

University and college libraries serve the research needs of scholars, students, and researchers, and they have a large number of professional-level books. Although many libraries limit their use to faculty and students, most will allow you a one-time use or allow you to buy a membership.

Company Libraries

Large companies such as the Automobile Club of Southern California, Twentieth Century-Fox motion picture studio, Hallmark Cards, Inc.

and Pillsbury Co. have extensive libraries, generally to help their employees perform their duties more efficiently. There may be a large company near you that can help you in your research.

Newspaper Libraries

Many large newspaper libraries have reference book and magazine collections for their staff to use in verifying information, and they have been known to allow others to use these resources. Check with the newspaper's editor or publisher.

Locating Special Libraries

The directories listed below identify libraries of every kind and can direct you in any research endeavor. The best place to locate these directories is – you guessed it – the library.

American Library Directory
Jaques Cattell Press/R.R.Bowker Co.
Lists more than 30,000 U.S. and Canadian libraries from hospital to zoo libraries.

Directory of Special Libraries and Information Centers
By Gale Research Co.
Five volumes.

Research Centers Directory
By Gale Research Co.

Directory of Historical Societies and Agencies in the U.S.and Canada
Lists historical and genealogical societies.

Subject Collection
Lee Ash/R.R. Bowker Co.
Lists 7,000 academic, public, museum, and historical society libraries nationwide.

Writer's Resource Guide
Edited by Bernadine Clark, Writer's Digest Books
Lists foundations, associations, and agencies, among others.

Other Sources of Information

- Hospitals and clinics
- Federal and state government agencies
- Consulates and embassies
- Chambers of commerce
- Trade professionals and hobby associations
- Periodicals
- Government documents
- On-line databases
- Local experts

Another interesting source for information is the *Index to How-To-Do-It Information*, Norman Lathrop Enterprises, which covers approximately 55 magazines that feature how-to articles.

Foreign Markets

For an excellent directory of merchants and manufacturers from around the world, review:

Kelly's Manufacturers and Merchants Directory
Kelly's Directory's Ltd.
Neville House
Eden Street
Kingston-On-Thames, KT11BY
Surrey, England

Directories

These resources, available to help inventors, are generally available at most libraries:

Directory of Corporate Affiliations
Standard & Poor Register of Corporations
Dun & Bradstreet Million Dollar Directory
Dun's Industrial Guide
Standard Directory of Advertisers
Trinet Establishment Database

International Directories

    International Directory of Corporate Affiliations

    Dun & Bradstreet Principal International Businesses

Manufacturers' Directories

    Thomas Register

    MacRae's Blue Book

    U.S. Industrial Directory

    State Directories

    Moody's Manuals

    Standard & Poor's Corporation Records

    Annual Reports

    10-K Report

Current Information

    Business Index

    Business Periodicals Index

    Predicast F & S Index

    The Wall Street Journal/Barron's Index

    U.S. Industrial Outlook

    Standard & Poor's Industry Surveys

    Oil Industry Comparative Appraisals

    Moody's Investor's Industry Review

Government Publications

    General Information Concerning Patents
    (Patent Office booklet)

    Attorneys and Agents Registered to Practice before the U.S. Patent & Trademark Office
    (Patent Office booklet)

    Index to the U.S. Patent Classification

    Manual of Classification

    Classification Definition

    Official Gazette of the U.S. Patent and Trademark Office

Databases

ABI/Inform
Contains general information on banking, finance, labor relations and sales management. Also includes business and related journals

F & S Index
Covers domestic and international companies, products, and information on new products.

Predicast
Forecasts for products, industries, and demographics.

Claims/U.S. Patent Abstract
Coverage from 1950 to the present.

Claims/Citation
References over five million patent numbers cited in U.S. patents since 1947.

World Patents Index
Patent coverage from 1963 to the present.

CA Search
Bibliographic information including patents, in chemical abstracts, from 1967 to the present.

Thomas New Industrial Products

PTS New Product Announcements

PTS Regional Business News

Business Dateline
(small business, start-ups)

Trade and Industry Index

Commerce Business Daily
(on-line version)

If you have a computer and modem and wish to do your own searches, contact:

Dialog Information Services, Inc.
3460 Hillview Avenue
Palo Alto, CA 94304
(800) 334-2564

Additional information can be obtained by using the county and city data books and the *Rand McNally Commercial Atlas and Marketing Guide* for regional buying incomes, retail sales information, and population centers.

While at the library you can also check out the *Commerce Business Daily* for contracts in your area of interest, and *Tech Notes*, a government publication on new innovation.

For information on financial support, contact the organizations below:

SBIR (Small Business Innovation Research) Grant Program
Office of Innovation, Research & Technology
U.S. Small Business Administration
1441 L Street, NW
Washington, DC 20416

Venture Capital Exchange
Enterprise Development Center
University of Tulsa
600 South College
Tulsa, OK 74104
(918) 592-6000, ext. 3152

Using Your Local University

Small Business Institutes (SBIs), organized through the U.S. Small Business Administration (SBA), are found at almost 500 university and college campuses nationwide.

At each SBI, senior and graduate students in the school of business administration and faculty advisors provide on-site management counseling. Students are guided by the faculty advisors and SBA management assistance experts, and receive academic credits for their research work. This can be a great help for those in-depth research projects.

Industrial Application Centers

Industrial application centers serve as technology utilization resources nationwide for industrial firms, individuals, agencies, public and private organizations, faculty and student personnel, and institutions concerned with the promotion of economic and technological developments. The main purpose of these centers is to help users of new technology obtain information appropriate to their needs.

Industrial application centers administer technology transfer through NASA's Technology Transfer Program. The technology available for transfer was all made through development programs of NASA and as such is made available for national use. For a nominal fee, or sometimes even at no cost, the centers will tie in to the extensive NASA database, allowing you access to literally millions of documents from worldwide sources.

Industrial application centers are generally associated with universities; they can also be located by contacting the Chamber of Commerce or your local library.

Industrial application centers can also access hundreds of other databases for in-depth research studies. I have used the local centers several times to obtain reports for many of my projects; all of the reports were provided at no cost.

You can obtain more information about these services by calling or writing the nearest industrial application center. This list helps you locate the center nearest you:

Industrial Application Centers

Indianapolis Center for Advanced Research
611 N. Capitol Avenue
Indianapolis, IN 46204
(317) 262-5036

Central Industrial Applications Center/NASA (CIAC)
P.O. Box 1335
Durant, OK 74702
(405) 924-5094
(800) 658-2823

Science and Technology Research Center (STRC)
P.O. Box 12235
Research Triangle Park
Durham, NC 27709-2235
(919) 549-0671

NASA Industrial Applications Center
823 William Pitt Union
University of Pittsburgh
Pittsburgh, PA 15260
(412) 648-7000

Southern Technology Applications Center
Box 24
Progress Center, One Progress Boulevard
Alachua, FL 32615
(904) 462-3913
(800) 354-4832 (FL only)
(800) 225-0308

NASA/UK Technology Applications Program
University of Kentucky
109 Kinkead Hall
Lexington, KY 40506-0057
(606) 257-6322

NERAC, Inc.
One Technology Drive
Tolland, CT 06084
(203) 872-7000

Technology Application Center (TAC)
University of New Mexico
Albuquerque, NM 87131
(505) 277-3622

NASA Industrial Application Center
University of Southern California
Research Annex
3716 South Hope Street
Los Angeles, CA 90007-4344
(213) 743-6132
(800) 642-2872 (CA only)
(800) 872-7477

NASA/SU Industrial Application Center
Southern University Department of Computer Science
P.O. Box 9737
Baton Rouge, LA 70813-9737
(504) 771-6272
(504) 771-4950

Other Sources Of Research

Center for the Utilization of Federal Technology
National Technical Information Service
5285 Port Royal Road
Springfield, VA, 22161

An important resource for new product development, NTIS is a central clearinghouse for public sale of government-sponsored research and development, foreign technology, and market data. NTIS offers computer searches through bibliographic databases.

Department of Commerce
Washington, D.C., 20234

The Department of Commerce will send you information on business and defense services needing new products.

Clearinghouse for Federal Scientific and Technical Information
Springfield, VA, 22151

This agency provides information on trends in specific industries, new scientific technical reports, marketing data, and new product information. When writing for information, request the Distribution Data Guide and Business Services Bulletins, which give information on products and services.

Also check with:

Small Business Administration (SBA)
P.O. Box 30
Denver CO. 80201-0030
(800) 368-5855

If you're researching alternative energy development, contact:

National Appropriate Technology Assistance Service
U.S. Department of Energy
P.O. Box 2525
Butte, MT 59702

The U.S. Department of Energy (DOE) can provide both information and technical assistance.

NOTES

NOTES

Chapter 5

Marketing

Marketing your new idea or product is one of the most important stages in becoming successful. For those confident of their ability, knowledge, and determination, taking an invention to the market will be a great adventure.

The reason so many inventors fail to get their ideas and concepts to the market is their inability to adequately comprehend the importance of each step involved. If you are serious about turning your creativity into profits, you must master or at least understand marketing.

Maybe up to now you were interested in making a better product or advancing technology. Maybe all you wanted to do was get rich quick, but none of that will happen until you attract customers. Understanding and targeting your customer is what marketing is all about. If your product satisfies a need or desire and the price is right, your job is so much the easier.

Marketing begins with a product idea (creativity), but successful marketing is complete when the product (your idea) is at the right place (distribution) at the right time (a little luck) at the right price (pricing), with effective communication to potential customers (sales promotion).

To have the right product at the right time, you must identify consumer needs or wants, preferences, and motivation. Become familiar with competitive products and activities, economic conditions, and government regulations. You must develop an intimacy with the market, understanding potential customers and how they think and act. Only then can you target your customer. Think of your customer as buying an expectation of benefits. The buyer wants satisfaction from your product; your goal is to satisfy that desire.

Preliminary Testing

One of the most common problems facing new products is inadequate testing in the marketplace. It isn't what the inventor or manufacturer thinks about the product that counts, but what the consumer thinks about the product.

The best way to test your product is to expose it to the public. There is a simple do-it-yourself test that you can perform if you know or have access to at least 20 people, preferably as many as 50. These people should not be relatives or close friends, as they have to be objective and totally honest.

This test is really quite simple. All you have to do is to show them your product and ask some basic questions, such as:

- How much would they pay for your product?

- Would they buy it, if the price was comparable to that of the competition?

- What type of product are they using now, and why?

Now start a file and store the data you obtain from these people until the testing is completed. Once you've collected data from at least 20 people, go over the information and see exactly how many people would purchase your product. If only 1 out of 20 said yes, you have some serious problems, either with your marketing methods or with the product itself. Re-evaluate your product.

Next, determine the power of your competitors by comparing notes on what product the people are currently using. Going up against a familiar product without having a unique feature people want and need could be considered marketing suicide.

Using your data, determine roughly how much people would pay for your product. To do this, average out the prices you were given.

Now, if you really want to put your product to a good marketing test, calculate its profit potential. Take the average price as determined in your survey and subtract: 25% for the retail mark-up (if it's a specialty item or is sold by hardware stores, subtract 40%); 10% for the cost of transporting the product to the store; 15% for advertising (if you intend to do any); 10% for warehousing; 5% for administration and your salary, and 5% for insurance. Once all of these costs are subtracted from the average retail price, you will see what is left to produce the product. If the numbers look reasonably good, you have a product that has some profit potential. If the numbers are negative, you'll have to work to correct this.

The table below is based on an item which, according to preliminary testing, should sell at retail for $10.

	Retail price	$10.00
−	(25%) Retail mark-up	<2.50>
=		$7.50
−	(10%) Transportation	<1.00>
=		$6.50
−	(15%) Advertising	<1.50>
=		$5.00
−	(10%) Warehousing	<1.00>
=		$4.00
−	(5%) Administration, Salary	<.50>
=		$3.50
−	Insurance	<.50>
=	Potential Profit	$3.00

If your product is a specialty item, the retail mark-up figure would be $4.00, and the potential profit would only be $1.50.

Now that you've displayed your product and received a preliminary response, it's time to try test marketing.

Test Marketing

Test marketing is the sampling of a limited quantity of products in the test marketplace. The results of a marketing test will tell you about sales potential, projected production needs, and profits. The test will produce preliminary data for determining how and where to market. You will have complimented the product by critique and evaluation. In one sense, you are experimenting to see what happens when the product is exposed to the consumer.

What Does the Consumer Think?

One very important purpose of the market test is to find out what the consumer thinks. To do that you must find the consumer, show the consumer your product, and then listen to his response. The results of your market test will be very important and should be taken seriously. The data should be used to make refinements in both your product and marketing efforts.

For example, an individual purchased a $10 license to become a street vendor to test his new product, and spent weekends on street corners testing his idea. He made about $800 a day selling the product out of his van. At the same time, he set up displays in local stores. In the stores, his product netted about $20 a week. He is now doing what his market test suggested and travels from town to town selling his product from his van. You never know where your market may be unless you experiment.

In test marketing, sometimes you have to show a little ambition and risk doing a little selling yourself. Anyone can sit at a flea market on the weekend, form his own marketing study, and have some fun in the process.

For those who may not feel comfortable sitting on a street corner, a more conventional approach would be to display your product in local store space, a competitive environment where established distributors make their living. The challenge is to make them move over.

In order to receive precious shelf space in the appropriate store, you will need to speak with either the store owner or manager to learn the requirements. A professional approach to this is to leave the product in the car and personally approach the owner or manager. Introduce yourself, and ask to set up an appointment to talk about a new product – your product. At the appointment, listen and learn. A manager can provide a wealth of marketing information; ask him about providing space for a test-market display and what you would need to do to conform to his store's requirements. Most managers have the authority to purchase directly from you and are usually willing to give a new product a chance, if it is properly packaged.

If you're going to sell your product from a store shelf or even a street corner, remember to use your imagination for unconventional and refreshing marketing angles. Continue to explore the data to determine what other directions you may also take.

Pricing

Some products are so similar and competition so well entrenched that industry pricing practices must be followed closely. Competition sets the price, and you, as a newcomer to the market, will generally want to sell at or below the competition's prices.

The strategy of making a better product and selling it for less than the competition is a good strategy only if the better product costs less to make than the competitor's product. There are three points to consider in pricing your product: demand, cost, and profit.

Demand orientation means prices are set by market forces. The inventor can influence demand through such things as product differences, services, and quality compared to competitive or substitute products.

Different product features and benefits can be offered to different market segments. Even with demand orientation, the consumer must perceive the value of the product to be higher than the price that must be paid for it.

Cost-oriented pricing is based upon considerations within the company, including the mark-up above the cost to produce. Mark-up pricing is most widely used because of its simplicity and ease of understanding. Mark-up pricing does not generally consider cost variations and the influence of demand for the product.

Mark-up pricing is generally used as a price limit, or a minimum price at which sales will be profitable. Many times a new market will start initial pricing by demand factors, sometimes referred to as "what the market will bear," later moving to mark-up pricing.

Profit-oriented pricing is based on price versus volume versus profit. Many times a breakeven analysis is used to consider fixed cost, variable cost, sales volume, and resulting profits from sales in order to skim as much profit off the top as possible.

Profit-oriented pricing is also known as skimming the market; this is when a product is introduced at a high price to take advantage of the high profits available from customers willing to pay a higher price to be first to own the product

After the cream of the market is taken, you then reduce the price to attract the mass market to the product and to meet new competition. The high profits obtained during the skimming phase will, of course, invite many competitors into the market.

One of the best examples of this type of marketing is the calculator business of the 1970s. My first calculator cost $69.95 and today that same calculator sells for about $6.

For additional information on pricing, examine these books:

> **Pricing Practices and Strategies**
> by Earl L. Bailey
> Published by The Conference Board, Inc.

> **Pricing Strategies**
> by Alfred R. Ovenfeldt
> Published by AMACOM

Marketing Assistance

Once your product is available to the public, enhance your chances of success through publicity. Publicity doesn't always mean prime time exposure or a television commercial. Actually, the best publicity for test marketing a product is free. There's an array of free advertisers out there just waiting to help you, if you know how to ask.

First, contact the local newspaper. Tell the reporter or editor that a local reader, inventor, or company is test marketing a new product. Normally, newspapers will not pass up a story of local interest.

The first article written about a business venture of my own produced more than 100 clients. Newspapers offer a great avenue to tell the world about what you're doing.

Next, call the local news stations and ask about a news story for your new product. Many cable television stations will broadcast commercials for your product on a percentage basis, which includes production costs. Normally, products of interest to these stations are the higher-profit items which sell for less than $24. For air time and production of the commercial, expect to give away at least 50% of the profit.

Talk to local radio stations about using public service announcements or local community spots. Use every possibility to expose your product and yourself; don't be shy. The publicity you create for yourself and your product will reach thousands of prospective customers, which in turn will mean greater profits.

A good friend of mine, Lee Mauck, invented the Res-Q-Ring, an innovative ring buoy. Lee discovered the importance of publicity when he found that Oklahomans, not having an ocean nearby, had little interest in his invention. So Lee devised a publicity stunt by renting a helicopter and jumping into the Arkansas River to be rescued by his new invention. He, of course, called the local television stations ahead of time and invited them to watch.

The publicity stunt worked so well that the local stations put the story on The Associated Press, where it was picked up by other stations across the country. Not only was the story seen nationwide, but Lee was invited to demonstrate his invention on the network TV show "That's Incredible."

The prime time exposure Lee received would have cost him hundreds of thousands of dollars had he paid for the air time. Instead, his product was launched to its ultimate success when investors called from around the country wishing to invest in the product. Most important, Lee believed in his invention enough to put his life on the line – he's a serious inventor who deserves his success.

Another publicity tool which can reach thousands of prospective customers is the magazine news release. To use this valuable tool, first write a good description of your product, listing all its features and benefits. Be sure and include your name, address, and phone number. If you do not have a business phone, you may wish to hire an answering service and use its number. Some telephone answering services start at only $25 per month and can be a wise investment. Some services will also take orders as well.

In order to determine your best possibilities for a suitable magazine, go to the library and review *The Writers Market* or the *Standard Rate and Data Service Book*, which lists some 12,000 publications including all the magazines within your particular market or industry.

You should further review the chapter on research for other publications. No matter what your invention's category there is probably a publication that covers it. Recently I found that the *Ballet News* is read by more than 30,000 people and that a magazine called *Bow and Arrow* has more than 100,000 readers each month. Other good sources are:

The Standard Periodical Directory
Oxbridge Publishing Co., Inc.
420 Lexington Avenue
New York, NY 10017

Ulrich's International Periodicals Directory
R.R. Bowker Co.
1180 Avenue of the Americas
New York, NY 10036

To properly approach these magazines, use a press release kit consisting of a cover letter explaining that you would like to be listed in the magazine's new product section, a description of the new product including features and benefits, and a sharp 5" x 7" black-and-white photo. Always send your kit to the attention of the editorial department and indicate on the envelope that dated material is enclosed.

If you do not have a black-and-white photograph of your product and do not wish to hire a professional photographer, you can take the photo yourself. Position your product in front of a white posterboard backdrop. The best shots can be obtained by using natural light; a low F stop setting on the camera will help obscure the background and draw attention to the product.

One last point to mention here is that some magazines may require several months lead time, and some magazines now charge to list your product within their new product sections. You must determine if the price for that publicity is reasonable for the coverage you may obtain.

Packaging Your Product to Sell

The last time you were in a store, did you notice the hundreds of products along the aisles? On any crowded shelf, did a particular product grab your attention? If so, you were most likely attracted by the packaging.

Often products are actually hidden away, tightly sealed within the confines of a box or package. If the packaging does not promote an immediate interest in the product, it is contributing to the failure of that product. Packaging can spell either success or failure for your product. Think what your response would be if you saw roses packaged in tin cans or a coat sold in a sealed box.

The first impression a prospective customer gets of your product is from the package. Visually, you must ensure quality and confidence in the product. Appropriate packaging will effectively display your product in its best light to a targeted market.

Since packaging contributes so much to your product's chance for success, you should consider professional assistance in designing your package. Packaging designers and industrial designers can be located in the Yellow Pages and can contribute significantly to the market appeal of your product.

If you are not in a position to hire an expert in packaging, you will find it beneficial to visit the library for information on marketing trends and studies (usually in the research and technical section).

Your package must present a clean, efficient, and attractive way of getting a product from the manufacturer to the consumer. There are many kinds of packaging to choose from, and the product itself usually has a way of determining the outcome.

Today's packages must not only be attractive, they must also be easy to load, resistant to damage, simple to pack and unpack for bulk shipment, and lightweight.

Packaging is important enough to be one of the largest categories of patents, and if you're doing a patent search, check class 229 for some unique packaging ideas.

If you're still not convinced of the importance of packaging, consider that Procter & Gamble invested millions of dollars in packaging

Pringles® potato chips, a product which had more advertising about the package than the product itself. The quality or novelty of packaging is an important factor in marketing consumer goods.

Another consideration is to make your packaging serve more than one purpose. Can your package be used as the display in the store? Will it deter shoplifters? Can it sit on a shelf as well as be hung on a peg?

Your packaged product should sell itself. Be innovative and enthusiastic about this area and gain a better chance for success. For further information on package design, read *The Silent Salesman: How to Develop Packaging that Sells* by James Pilditch, published by Beckman Publishers.

A Professional Approach

In the same way you package a product to sell, you must also package yourself to sell. Professionals like dealing with other professionals. Being businesslike will increase your chances of success tenfold over being a nonprofessional.

An inventor once came to me complaining that he never received a reply from his letters to manufacturers. In talking with him, I learned that he was hand writing his letters on notebook paper. Furthermore, the letters were not sent to the attention of a specific person.

I explained that he was wasting time, and that his letters were most likely being trashed by the first secretary to open them. Quite simply, his letters gained little or no respect in the business world. If an inventor expects to be treated professionally, he must act professionally.

After explaining to the inventor that business people rarely consider inventors to have good sales potential, we resubmitted the letter. Instead of hand writing a letter, we typed out a request for a quote. We used his business letterhead, which is discussed in more detail below. We even had the letter meter-stamped at the post office to give it that professional look.

This inventor not only received a prompt reply, but also a company catalog, sale ads, and free samples, all of which resulted from creating a professional appearance.

If you wish to come up with some inexpensive letterhead to use for your correspondence, go to the local art store or business supply store and purchase some rub-on letters, also known as dry transfer lettering. A sheet will usually cost about $5. Pick a professional-looking style you like and apply your company name, address, and telephone number on a clean 81/2" x 11" sheet of paper. It may take a couple of tries to master the art of using rub-on letters but generally it's pretty easy. Creating your own letterhead is only another avenue for using your creative talent and adding to your professional approach.

If you own a personal computer or have access to one, you can design your letterhead using any one of several graphics software programs .

Once you have your personal letterhead, go to a local printer or copy shop and run off some copies on good quality paper and store the original for future use. You now have a "company" letterhead.

If you don't have a company name, make one up. Having a company name to do business under costs little or nothing. You do not have to incorporate a company to use a business name. While some states require that you register a company name, the cost is usually minimal.

In choosing a name for your business, consider the importance of the name. A name like Barney and Charlie's Inventions may not sound professional, while using the initials and calling the business the BCI Company would certainly sound more professional and garner more respect.

I can remember naming a company ADP Enterprises (after my wife's initials) and later having to change the meaning of the acronym to Automated Protection Devices when the company grew. It was a good thing the product line we were selling matched the initials in the new acronym.

Professional Use of the Phone

Many inventors are not used to dealing with large companies – this can be apparent when they use the telephone. When the person you need is not available, leave a number where you can be reached. Constantly calling someone until you reach them is unprofessional.

It's always a good idea to keep notes of every phone conversation. Write down the who, when, and where of your conversations; an inventor's log book is the best place to keep this information. Treat every phone contact as though he or she is very important. In general, remember to act professionally and businesslike with every opportunity, and always think success.

Trademarks, Logos, and Brand Names

An important factor in successful packaging is the proper use and design of your company identity. For example, think about such names as the First Security National Bank, Great Northern Railroad, or Transcontinental Airlines. These names reflect a powerful and imposing nature, in the same way names like Bud's Hot Dog Stand, Whiz Bang Plumbers, or Frank's Bar and Grill imply a totally different feel, even though they may be appropriate for what they do.

Now, when we mix them up a little and get names like The First National Hot Dog Stand, Frank's Bank, and Whiz Bang Airlines, we see how a name can imply a feeling about the product and even the company behind the product.

Your company name should be appropriate to your product line, easy to read and, most importantly, easy to remember. An easily identifiable and attractive logo, brand name, or company name will add substantially to repeat sales and integrity, and will promote familiarity, confidence, and appeal in the product.

When your logo or brand name is created, it's a good idea to file for a trademark. This is covered in more detail in Chapter 2. A trademark will give immediate protection for your logo or brand name and can be important for future licensing possibilities. Many states only charge $25 to $50 for state trademark protection, and you may obtain the needed form by calling the secretary of state's office.

You should seek professional assistance when designing your logo. If that option is not available, I recommend a trip to the library or book store to study such topics as color selection for marketing appeal, design symmetry, style selection, and current marketing trends. Other study aids include clip-art books and printers' paste-up books.

It can also be very enlightening to look at different logos and packaging layouts used for goods already on store shelves. Remember, most of these packages have cost the companies using them thousands of dollars to develop and test.

Other sources for ideas on trademarks, logos, and brand names include:

Why Did They Name It?
By Hannah Campbell
Published by Fleet Press

The Name Game: How to Name a Company or Product
By Henri Charmasson
Published by Dow Jones-Irwin

Entrepreneurs: The Men and Women Behind Famous Brand Names and How They Made It
By Joseph J. and Suzy Fucini
Published by G.K. Hall

The Company Image: Building Your Identity and Influence in the Marketplace
By Elinor Selame
Published by Wiley Press

Trade Shows

Another topic deserving special attention is the trade show. There are more than 8,000 trade shows each year in the United States alone, catering to every industry from toys to automobiles.

Booth space for various shows ranges from $50 to thousands of dollars for such megacenters as the McCormick Center in Chicago.

Many success stories come from trade shows, like the two women who spent $500 on a booth to promote slip-free socks at a children's-wear show and made $10,000 in one day, or the owner of Contemporary Designs, who wrote over $14,000 in orders in just one day at a boutique show in New York City.

Trade shows put thousands of potential customers in one place, willing and seeking to buy new products. Many beginning companies use trade show successes to finance their start-up costs as well as to support their marketing studies.

Many trade shows now assign booth locations by the lottery method, and you may find your booth at the front door or next to your biggest competitor with its high-tech, expensive booth which makes your booth look inferior.

Before you attend a trade show, visit a professional display maker, if not to purchase, at least to look at a professionally made booth. Projecting a company image is very important at trade shows, and the impression you leave will stay with potential customers.

An important marketing tip to mention here is to have some kind of advertising giveaway or gimmick. Small samples are always very effective whenever possible, but even if it's a printed key chain, use the opportunity to develop return customers.

Shown on the following pages is a partial list of trade shows and their approximate dates. For a more comprehensive list, write for the *Annual Directory of Trade and Industrial Shows*, available through *Successful Meeting Magazine*, Directory Department, 633 Third Avenue, New York, NY 10017, or refer to the *Directory of North American Fairs, Festivals and Expositions*, P.O. Box 24970, Nashville, TN 37202. Both are available at most larger libraries.

January Shows

California Gift Show
Los Angeles Convention Center
Contact: AMC Trade Shows
1933 South Broadway
Los Angeles, CA 90007
(213) 747-3488

Portland Gift Show
Portland, Oregon
Contact: Western Exhibitors
2181 Greenwich Street
San Francisco, CA 94123
(415) 346-6666

Atlanta National Gift & Accessories Market
Atlanta Merchandise Mart
Contact: National Market Center
240 Peachtree Street NW, #2200
Atlanta, GA 30303
(404) 220-2123

International Fashion Boutique Show
Jacob K. Javits Convention Center, New York City
Contact: Larkin-Pluznick-Larkin
100 Wells Avenue
Newton, MA 02159
(617) 964-5100

Fashion Accessories Expo
New York City
Contact: Accessories Magazine
50 Day Street, 4th Floor
Norwalk, CT 06854
or call Conference Management Corp., (203) 582-0500

Beckman's Gift Show
Los Angeles Sports Arena
For handcrafted gift items
Contact: Industry Productions of America
P.O. Box 27337
Los Angeles, CA 90027
(213) 962-5424

International Kids' Fashion Show
Jacob K. Javits Convention Center, New York City
Contact: Larkin-Pluznik-Larkin
71 West 35th Street, #1600
New York, NY 10001
(212) 594-0880
in California, call (213) 623-SHOW

National Business Opportunity Shows
Portland, Oregon Memorial Coliseum
Contact: SC Promotions
730 East Market Street
Long Beach, CA 90805
(213) 428-7660

Charlotte Gift Show
Charlotte, North Carolina, Merchandise Mart
Contact: Mahone Associates
D-328 Charlotte Merchandise Mart
2500 E. Independence Boulevard
Charlotte, NC 28205
(704) 377-5881

PGA Merchandise Show
Orlando, Florida
Contact: PGA of America
100 Avenue of Champions
Palm Beach Gardens, FL 33418
(407) 624-8400

National Association of Men's Sportswear Buyers
Jacob K. Javits Convention Center, New York City
Contact: Schimel Co., Inc.
535 5th Avenue, 27th Floor
New York, NY 10017
(212) 986-1811

Cincinnati Travel, Sports & Boat Show
Dr. Albert B. Sabine Convention Center, Cincinnati, Ohio
For exhibitor information, contact: Hart Productions Inc.
1251 Kemper Meadow Drive, #400
Cincinnati, OH 45240-1633
(513) 825-1600

Spring West Action Sports Retailer Trade Expo
San Diego, Calif.
Contact: Pacifica Publishing Corp.
P.O. Box 348
South Laguna, CA 92677
(714) 499-5374.

February Shows

Salt Lake Gift Show
Salt Lake City, Utah
Contact: Progressive Exhibitors Inc.
424 South 700 East
Salt Lake City, UT 84102
(801) 363-GIFT

Southern Sign Show
Charlotte Convention Center
Contact: The National Electric Sign Association
801 N. Fairfax Street
Alexandria, VA 22314,
(703) 836-4012

The Super Show
Georgia World Congress Center, Atlanta
Includes the New Product Show
Contact: The Super Show
1450 NE 123rd Street
North Miami, FL 33161
(800) 327-3736
in Florida, (305) 893-8771

Sunstate Gift Show
Curtis Hixon Convention Center, Tampa, Fla.
Contact: Atlanta Market Center
240 Peachtree Street, #2200
Atlanta, GA 30303
(404) 220-2205

American International Toy Fair
Jacob K. Javits Convention Center, New York City
For a brochure, write: Toy Manufacturers of America Inc.
200 Fifth Avenue
New York, NY 10010

Variety Merchandise Show
Jacob K. Javits Convention Center, New York City
Contact: Thalheim Exposition Inc.
42 Bayview Avenue
P.O. Box 4200
Manhasset, NY 11030-4200
(516) 627-4000

Business Opportunities Expo
San Mateo Center, San Mateo, Calif., and
Los Angeles Convention Center, Los Angeles
Contact: Spectrum Shows Inc.
Santa Barbara, CA
(805) 563-9118

New York International Gift Fair
Jacob K. Javits Convention Center, New York City
Contact: George Little Management Inc.
2 Park Avenue, #1100
New York, NY 10016
(212) 686-6070

March Shows

International franchising shows
Vancouver Trade & Convention Center, Vancouver, British Columbia,
and CNE Exhibition Place's Automotive Building Toronto, Ontario
Contact: PROMEXPO
30 St. Patrick Street, #301
Toronto, Ontario, Canada M5T 3A3
(416) 971-9526

Money Expo
Madison Square Garden, New York City
Contact: Money Expo Inc.
1784 Fifth Avenue
Bay Shore, NY 11706
(516) 434-1060

America's Family Pet Show
Pomona, Calif.
Contact: American Pet Society
P.O. Box 1337
South Pasadena, CA 91031-1337
(818) 799-7220

The National Business Opportunities Show
Arlington Convention Center, Arlington, Texas
Contact: SC Promotions
730 E. Market Street
Long Beach, CA 90805
(213) 428-7660.

April Shows

Industrial Shows of America
For information, write to: 20 W. Alyesbury Road
Timonium, MD 21093
(800) 638-6396

The Automotive Aftermarket Show
For information, write or call: 150 Burling Avenue
Chicago, IL 60514
(312) 850-7779

Wholesale To Go Show
For information, write to 1100 Brandywine Boulevard
BX2188
Zanesville, OH 43702

May Shows

Sunstate Gift Show
For information, write to: 240 Peachtree Street, Suite 2200
Atlanta, GA 30303

The Business and Office Expo
For information, write or call: 1552 Hertel Avenue
Buffalo, NY 14216
(716) 834-9431

Electrical Industry Show
For information, write or call: 4930 W. 77th Street, Suite 150
Minneapolis, MN 55435
(612) 835-4808

June Shows

Southern California Expo
For information, write or call: 2260 Jimmy Durante Boulevard
Del Mar, CA 92014
(619) 755-1161

July Shows

American Gift and Art Show
For information, write or call: 100 Bickford
Rochester, NY 14606
(716) 254-2580

National Gift Market
For information, write: 240 Peachtree Street, NW, Suite 2200
Atlanta, GA 30043

August Shows

The Gift and Decorative Show
For information, write or call: 1100 Brandywine Boulevard, BX2188
Zanesville, OH 43702
(614) 452-4541

San Francisco Gift Show
For information, write or call: 2181 Greenwich Street
San Francisco, CA 94123
(415) 346-6666

Calgary Gift Show
For information, write: 6143 West Willow Drive, Suite 100
Englewood, CO 80111

September Shows

Charlotte Housewares Show
For information, write or call:
2500 East Independence Boulevard, D-328
Charlotte, NC 28205
(704) 377-5881

Southern Ideal Home Show
For information, write or call: Box 36859
Charlotte, NC 28236
(800) 334-0248

October Shows

Hardware Wholesalers Show
For information, write or call: Box 868, Nelson Road
Fort Wayne, IN 46801
(219) 749-8531

Fish Expo

For information, write or call: 5 Milk Street
Box 7437 DTS
Portland, ME 04112
(207) 772-3005

November Shows

Christmas Gift Show

For information, write or call: Box 333
Eagle, ID 83616
(800) 635-2274

Additional shows beneficial for showing new products include:

Invention Convention

Contact: International Convention Services
1645 N. Vine Street, Suite 611
Hollywood, CA 90028

Inventech Expo

Contact: Inventors Workshop International
Education Foundation
3537 Old Conejo Road, Suite 120
Newbury Park, CA 91320

National Inventors' Week Exposition

Contact: U.S. Patent & Trademark Office
Washington, DC 20231

New Product Technology Development Conference

For information, write to: P.O. Box 12793
Research Triangle Park, NC 27709.

International Conventions

For information on some international inventors' conventions, write to
the addresses below:

International Exposition of Inventions

Messezentrum Nuremberg
D-8500 Nuremberg 50
Germany

Business World Exhibition
1801 McGill College Avenue, Suite 970
Montreal, Quebec H3A2N4
Canada

Hannover Fair
Deutsche Messe-und Ausstellungs-AG
Messegelande
D-300 Hannover
Germany

Techno Tokyo
Promotion Division
Nihon Cogyo Jimbocho
Chiyoda-ko
Tokyo, 101
Japan

Inova
S.A. Technoexpo
8 Rue de la Michodiere
75002 Paris
France

International Exposition Inventions
Secretariat du Salon, 8
Rue du 31 Decembre
Geneva, CH-1207
Switzerland

Flanders Technology International
International Jaarbeurs
Van Vlaanderen VZW
ICC Floraliaplaeis B-9000, Ghent
Belgium

European Fairs and Corresponding U.S. Contacts

HANNOVER

Hannover Fairs USA, Inc.
P.O. Box 7066
103 Carnegie Center
Princeton, NJ 08540

MUNICH

Kallman and Associates
5 Maple Court
Ridgewood, NJ 07450
(201) 652-7070

DUSSELDORF

Dusseldorf Trade Shows, Inc.
Empire State Building, Suite 4621
New York, NY 10018
(212) 239-3750

FRANKFURT AND COLOGNE

German-American Chamber of Commerce, Inc.
Trade Fairs Department
666 Fifth Avenue
New York, NY 10103
(212) 974-8830

BERLIN

AMK Berlin
101 W. Grand Avenue
Suite 601
Chicago, IL 60610
(312) 245-5230

MILAN

Delia Associates
Milan Fairs USA
P.O. Box 338
Route 22
West Whitehouse, NJ 08888
(201) 534-9044

For further updated information on European trade fairs, there are several publications available from the U.S. Department of Commerce, including:

European Trade Fairs: A Guide for Exporters (No charge)

German Trade Fairs: A Handbook for American Exhibitors and Exporters (Cost $4.50)

Europe Now (No Charge)

To request these publications, write to:

U.S. Department of Commerce
Publication Distribution
Room H1617M
Washington, DC 20230

In addition, The Oasis Press/PSI Research publishes a comprehensive guide to exporting. The book, *Export Now: A Guide for Small Businesses*, by Richard L. Leza, is available by calling (800) 228-2275.

Information for Exhibitors

For further information on setting up exhibits, here are some publications worth sending for:

Trade Shows and Exhibits
by Donald G. Stewart
Available from Association of National Advertisers
115 East 4th Street
New York, NY 10017

Great Show Exhibits
Designers and Producers Association
521 Fifth Avenue
New York, NY 10017

Sources for Locating Trade Associations

Directory of European Associations
Gale Research Co.
2200 Book Tower
Detroit, MI 48226
Lists more than 7,000 associations throughout Europe.

Encyclopedia of Associations
Gale Research Co.
2200 Book Tower
Detroit, MI 48226
Lists more than 16,000 national and regional associations.

National Trade and Professional Associations of the United States
Columbia Books, Inc.
917 15th Street, NW, Suite 300
Washington, DC 20005
Lists more than 4,300 national associations.

Long-Term Marketing

Consider that 50% of the consumer products now on the shelves were not there five years ago. The average life span of a consumer product is only about five years, and if you do not improve your product, someone else will. Of the products currently available for consumer use, only 25% will survive more than five years.

One fact which inventors do not consider in the beginning is that when marketing slows down, so do profits. When starting out, consider the long-range plans that must accompany the excitement of seeing your product on the shelf. Remember, profits and only profits keep distributors, store owners, and manufacturers happy.

When marketing your product, be thinking of new ideas for improvements and derivative products. If you have already established a place in the market, use it to explore new products which may have the same potential. You may even be able to help another inventor get to the market. According to the latest marketing statistics, if your company only makes one product, you may have less than a 3% chance of success. Remember, marketing is finding out what people want and giving them more of it.

One effective way of predicting future marketing trends is to read as many trade publications as possible. A company's success on the market may even be enhanced by updating its packaging to reflect new trends. For example, I worked with a company making an elaborate fishing-lure carrying case. After exploring the market, the company changed its focus to the medical industry. The company did so after discovering that paramedics were in need of specialized carrying cases similar to the one the company was already making for the fishing industry. The medical industry was also an easier market to target.

Always remain flexible and listen to market demand. Your survival depends upon it.

Terms and Standards Used in Industry

An important part of marketing is offering a quality product. Many times we find our own manufacturing resources limited and have to use outside sources to produce our product in larger quantities. When this happens, we have to depend upon others to supply quality products. In order to assure this, we need to speak the same language. The following are a few of the more commonly used terms in industry:

Standard Industry Classification (SIC) Numbers — In order to maintain some uniformity of data, states, counties, cities, and private sector directories and publications have adopted the United States method of identifying industry by using SIC Numbers. These numbers identify companies by industry category and range from two-digit to eight-digit numbers.

The two-digit numbers are used to designate basic industries such as mining, chemicals, and agriculture. As the number of digits increases, so does the detail of identification. The eight-digit number and the NEC (Not Elsewhere Classified) sections specifically list product categories. Many local government and private sector directories will vary the number of identifying digits. A company might have one or more SIC numbers.

You can use SIC numbers to identify similar industries and similar companies. The U.S. Department of Commerce and the Bureau of the Census publish handbooks explaining the SIC numbers and how to use them. You can also find them at the library.

Pantone Matching System — One industry standard you'll use in any color selection will be the Pantone Matching System (PMS) standard. PMS serves as an international color standard for selecting color.

For example, if I called for Pantone 3395 C as a product color, the manufacturer would know I wanted a green which was 71/2 parts Pantone Green, 1/2 part Pantone Yellow and 8 parts Pantone Transparent White, or, in percentages, 46.9% green, 3.1% yellow, and 50% transparent white. This procedure leaves no room for error and your product will be exactly the color you selected. Pantone Color Formula Guides are available at most art supply stores.

Other Standards

If you have a product which is flexible in any way, and if you wish to detail the exact hardness of the material, you would use either the Rockwell or Brinnell standards, or the Durometer for flexible materials.

For machine threads of screws and bolts we rely on "SAE" and "ISO" standards. If your product is used by the government or military, you will probably have to build to "MIL" specifications. When indicating a surface finish you should use "RMS" standards.

The reason for having such precise measurements in industry is simple. If two pieces must fit precisely, the possibility of a misfit is 50/50. If 10 parts must fit precisely, the possibility for error increases considerably. This is known as the "fault tree" in design engineering.

Selling to Department Stores

In order to deal directly with the larger department stores, you must have a comprehensive business plan. The department store buyer will want to know who is going to manufacture your product, who your vendor is, and in what quantities you are going to make the product. Do you have a cost analysis available which details how much it takes to make the product, what the profits to the representative are, and how much your profit is? In general, you must be able to show, from beginning to end, each stage of the product. (See Chapter 6 for information on preparing a business plan.)

You'll find many department stores will usually deal only with manufacturers or agents on their approved list. If you do not have proper representation or a manufacturer ready to produce your product, it will take longer to get in to see someone, if you get in at all.

If a department store accepts your product, you must be able to supply it with sizeable quantities in a short period of time.

Many new products fall in the housewares category, so if you do not have a vendor but one is required, you can obtain a list of manufacturers and vendors in your area. Write to:

National Housewares Manufacturers Association
1324 Merchandise Mart
Chicago, IL 60654

Distribution

The methods used in moving your product from production to consumption are key external sources that can affect your pricing, sales volume, and success.

There are three main types of distribution:

Direct marketing — The manufacturer sells directly to the consumer through his own sales force.

One-level distribution — Typically a retailer, sales agent, or manufacturer sells directly to a retail outlet.

Two-level distribution — The product moves through a wholesaler and then a retailer, or in industrial marketing, a sales agent and a wholesaler or distributor.

You may be wondering why a manufacturer would use so many middlemen, risking a loss of profits and control. Middlemen are used because of their efficiency and the increased distribution they give a product. Because of their experience, specialization, contacts, and scale of operation, they can distribute your product for less money than you could yourself.

The factors in creating good distribution include:

- Researching information for planning and facilitating exchange;
- Promoting the product (distributors often provide this service);
- Contacting prospective buyers;
- Matching your product to a buyer's requirements such as grading, assembling, packaging, financing, and the like;

- Negotiation of price and terms;

- Distributing (the transportation and storage of the product);

- Financing (sometimes included by the distributor serving as an agent for collecting and dispersal of funds); and

- Risk taking (also included because the product is out of your hands and has yet to be sold).

In evaluating which type of distribution is best for you, consider that when the number of customers is large and geographically dispersed, and when customers tend to buy in small quantities on a frequent basis, you should use long channels of distribution with many middlemen at each level.

Products that are bulky in relation to their value require channels that minimize the shipping distance and number of middlemen handling the product.

Usually the best reason for using middlemen is to transfer some very specific tasks including:

- Transit of goods;

- Advertising to inform and influence buyers;

- Storage of inventory from which orders are filled; and

- Searching out and communicating with buyers.

Selection of middlemen is an extremely important function and should be done carefully. To evaluate the distributor's potential, look at his years in business, growth record, cooperativeness, and overall reputation.

Communicating with the Consumer

Marketing is communication, and in order to communicate with your prospective customer you must consider one or more of these methods:

Advertising — A paid form of impersonal presentation and promotion;

Publicity — News about the product published in trade journals, newspapers, or broadcast on television and radio;

Sales Promotion — Trade shows, conventions, product literature; and

Personal Selling — Discussions with and presentations to consumers in person or by phone.

Advertising is used to create awareness of the product – its features and benefits – and to create a desire to purchase. Advertising motivates the consumer to see, buy, use, or gain additional information about the product.

Advertising should demonstrate the product and its benefits. Too much glitz and the product gets lost. Even if your product has a dozen features, list only the best two or three. Later, you can display all your features on the packaging, but a long list of features in an ad will lose the reader's attention quickly. The same holds true for publicity.

Product sales literature, on the other hand, should be both factual and dramatized. It should contain all the information that will help the prospective customer make a decision. Good sales literature will include highlights of features, performance data, specifications, photographs, and illustrations that will help the prospect evaluate your product.

It should also contain ordering information, a company address, telephone numbers, and where the product can be purchased.

Effective personal selling usually consists of informing the customers and helping them buy. It should be honest and straightforward. No matter how you approach the consumer, if they have a real need for the product, and you have the right price, at the right place, at the right time, the prospect will buy.

Marketing Cons

In getting your product to the market you may be enticed by a number of companies promoting themselves as invention brokers or marketing experts. And marketing experts they are, collectively making as much as $500 million a year. Unfortunately, this money is made preying on people who need marketing and development assistance.

These companies usually advertise in tabloids, on the radio or late-night television programs, and in magazines. The names change so often that there is no use in listing them. Many have tried to stop these companies, but as long as there are people willing to pay, they are here to stay, providing phony marketing services which can cost up to $20,000.

Some of the warning signs to look for in spotting these marketing scams include free evaluations; recommending further development while at the same time praising the product; refusal to work on commission; refusal to disclose other clients; and refusal to discuss the company or its background.

Often they will imply that the patent office disclosure document program offers patent protection. Once you've spotted a con marketing company, your best course of action is to simply stay away and warn others. Attempted legal action against any of these companies is totally worthless due to present laws on such matters.

One such con artist laid his trap in Tulsa, Oklahoma, where I currently live. He tricked 32 inventors into paying cash to him. By the time warrants were issued for his arrest, he was gone.

It's unfortunate that some very creative people have to pay someone to do what they could have done themselves and wind up losing their life savings.

Marketing Success Secrets

For increasing your chances of success, I can't emphasize enough the importance of understanding your market and acquiring all the knowledge you can gain.

The best and most inexpensive way to gain an edge in marketing is through reading as much material as possible on the subject. I have never read a book I felt was a waste of time. There is always something to be learned by reading; it's how you use it that's important.

The list below represents only a fraction of the existing information available for your use:

Marketing Newsletters

New Product News
Dancer Fitzgerald Sample
405 Lexington Avenue
New York, NY 10174

International New Product Newsletter
6 St. James Avenue
Boston, MA 02116

Selling to the Government

General Services Administration
Federal Supply Service
1734 New York Avenue, NW
Washington, DC 20406

Licensing Guidelines

Licensing Industry Mechanizers Association
Suite 303E
200 Park Avenue
New York, NY 10166

Mailing Lists

Dunhill Marketing Guide to Mailing Lists
Dunhill International
444 Park Avenue South
New York, NY 10016

Compilers Plus, Inc.
466 Main Street
New Rochelle, NY 10801

America Business Information
5711 S. 86th Circle
P.O. Box 27347
Omaha, Nebraska 68127

Standard Rate & Data Service
3004 Glenview Road
Wilmette, IL 60091-9970

Magazines

Advertising Age
Crown Communication, Inc.
740 Rush Street
Chicago, IL 60611
Has a feature entitled Idea Marketplace

Thomas Publications
1 Pennsylvania Plaza
New York, NY 10001
Has feature called Technology Mart for showing new ideas

Books

If you're interested in direct mail marketing, you will want to read at least one of the following books.

Mail Order Legal Manual
By Erwin J. Keup
Published by PSI Research/The Oasis Press
300 North Valley Drive
Grants Pass, OR 97526
The Oasis Press also offers books on many of the different aspects of business. You may receive a catalog by calling (800) 228-2275.

How to Start and Operate a Mail Order Business
By Julian L. Simon
Published by McGraw-Hill

Direct Marketing: Strategy, Planning, Execution
By Edward L. Nash
Published by McGraw-Hill

Building a Mail Order Business: A Complete Manual for Success
By William A. Cohen
Published by Wiley Press

Other Sources of Information

For other resources send for these guides:

> **County and City Data Book**
> **Directory of Federal Technology Transfer**
> **Commerce Business Daily**
> **Guide for the Submission of Unsolicited Research and Development Proposals**
> **How to Keep in Touch with U.S. Government Publications**
> **Monthly Catalog of United States Government Publications**

These guides are available from:

> **Superintendent of Documents**
> Government Printing Office
> Washington, DC 20402
> (202) 783-3238

Business Statistics

Other useful guides are available from the:

> **Small Business Administration**
> P.O. Box 30
> Denver, CO 80201-0030
> (800) 368-5855

Titles to ask for include:

> **Market Research Procedures**
> **Free Management Assistance Publication**
> **Basic Business Reference Sources**
> **Marketing for Small Business**
> **New Product Development**
> **Ideas into Dollars: A Resource Guide for Inventors and Innovative Small Businesses**

For Toy Inventors

> **Playthings Magazine**
> 51 Madison Avenue
> New York, NY 10010

Toys, Hobbies and Crafts
545 Fifth Avenue
New York, NY 10017

Toy Inventors of America
5813 McCart Avenue
Fort Worth, TX 76133
A toy inventors association

Toy Manufacturers of America, Inc.
Room 700
200 Fifth Avenue
New York, NY 10010

For Safety Requirements
Consumer Product Safety Commission
Washington, DC 20207.

For Showing Inventions
The Invention Trade Center
121 North Fir Street
Ventura, CA 93001
Exhibits inventions for six months for a fee.

NOTES

Chapter 6

Financing

The Business Plan

It has been said that a person without a plan is a person planning to fail. The business plan is your blueprint for success. If you plan to stay in business, you must have goals; goals and a plan of action are basic components of a business plan. I could give a dozen reasons why you need a business plan, but the most important reason is your desire to succeed.

Even if you never intend to talk to a venture capitalist or bank, and even if you don't intend to make a lot of money, you still need a solid plan to guide you. The business plan will identify and quantify your business, goals, objectives and time frame. Without goals, you're lost.

Planning Your Success

A sound business plan requires an investment in both time and resources. A business plan is not just an array of information: it's a guide which has been thoroughly researched; it's your map to indicate where you're going and how you're going to get there.

Before starting your business plan, you will need to clarify some points which you may have only vaguely considered up to now.

Consider these questions:

- What exactly is your product?
- What are your goals?
- Have you given your product a fair evaluation?
- Who is helping you in your business?
- Do you really understand your market?

- How big and where is your market?

- How will you approach your market?

- How much do you intend to spend on advertising?

- What are you willing to do to stay in business?

- Are you burning your bridges behind you?

How to Prepare a Business Plan

There is no single format which must be followed to the letter when it comes to business plans. But there is a format which is typical of most successful plans, and you can add to or delete from that format as required. Every business plan should contain: the executive summary, business history, the product analysis, the market analysis, an analysis of the competition, a marketing approach, manufacturing report, operation management analysis, and financial projections.

Getting Down To Business

The guidelines below will assist you in answering important questions and laying out your business plan. Even if a topic does not seem to fit your present needs, you should consider including it for future reference when your company begins to expand.

General Introduction

Write a paragraph or two as if you were explaining to a total stranger what your business does. Include the unique features of your product or company. Also include a projection of the future of your business and a report on where your customers are now and where they'll be in the future.

The Executive Summary

This should be the serious sales pitch; it is where you describe the need for your product and business. The executive summary should be a two- to five-page overview designed to draw attention. If you are using the business plan to obtain financing, the executive summary will be the first thing a venture capitalist will read.

The executive summary should include a description of your product and business, target market, advantages over the competition, and who's running the business. Emphasize any special skills and experience of anyone within the organization. Provide a summary of financial projections for the next three to five years, where the capital to approach the market is coming from, and how it's going to be used.

Business History

The business history should include when the business was founded, its progress, a brief description of the founders, and the type of organization of the business such as incorporation or partnership. State who makes decisions, and why.

If yours is a new business with no history, describe your personal or professional background and experience that relate to the business. If a prospective investor is your target, show why the new business has a chance of becoming successful.

The Product

Explain precisely what the product is and why it is better than that of the competition. Explain how the product came to be and whether any other products are on the drawing board.

Detail production stages and costs. Is the product difficult to make? Is a skilled labor force required? Do you intend to use contract labor, hire your own, or hire the disabled? Where are the suppliers located, and are there additional suppliers in your area, in the event your source goes out of business?

Explain in detail any patents, trademarks, or copyrights; packaging designs; research and development costs still outstanding; special equipment needed, and any pending or received approvals such as Underwriters' Laboratories (U.L.) or factory mutual (F.M.) label.

Marketing

This is where you really need to shine. Include a comprehensive description of your present market, if any, and any market research available. Include your forecast for sales and your intended sales approach. Define who your customers are, and a five-year buying pattern. How will you distribute to the market? What has been done to test the market? Are there any liabilities? Is the product guaranteed and what insurance is required to sell it?

The marketing section of your business plan should be detailed and researched; without a useable marketing plan, the potential of your business can appear weak. Provide information on channels of distribution, a sales compensation plan (who gets what percentage to ensure sales), your pricing strategy and its comparison with others, promotional concepts, advertising, and the cost of advertising. How do you intend to monitor the market and stay ahead of it?

The Competition

It's important to know who you're going up against. Have you researched the strengths and weaknesses of your competition? Include literature on competitors' ads in the business plan; use graphs or charts to show their weaknesses. Be realistic. Don't assume your new product can compete as well as you would like. Anticipate problems.

Manufacturing Your Product

Are you making it? Is it being privately labeled or "shopped out?" How is quality control guaranteed? What are future projections if sales rise? Describe your experience in manufacturing.

Management

Describe the directors, officers, and employees, if any. Include resumes. Do you use any consultants, accountants, attorneys, or bankers? Include job descriptions of key personnel and compensation paid to each of these individuals. Include as many strong points as possible about the team and yourself.

Financial Projections

Your financial projection is important to a prospective investor because it indicates how much money you need and when you need it. It also tells the investor when he or she will be paid back. At a minimum, you should include a balance sheet, profit and loss statement, expected source and application of funds, profit and loss projections, and a cash flow projection. You should, if possible, include either five years of history or three to five years of projections. Obviously, the financial projections must tie to data included elsewhere in your business plan.

Additional information for an ideal business plan would include an evaluation of management experience and capability, an evaluation of the choice of the form of business, an outline of personnel policy, an outline of your recordkeeping system, a review of the risk and your plans to cope with unexpected problems, and your pricing philosophy. Also include your merchandising plan, credit policy, space layout plan, estimate of breakeven sales based on profit projections, and even an opening-day balance sheet.

Your business plan will serve two important purposes. It will guide your actions and those on your team, and it will persuade prospective investors that you have a concept that merits serious consideration.

Funding Innovation

There are various sources from which you can obtain capital, and while each has its own benefits and faults, many times it's your particular situation which will warrant where your first attempt may be directed to receive start-up money or investment capital. Here is an overview of each of the different means available:

Family, Friends, and Savings — In the earliest stages of development, you may find it easier to obtain financial assistance from family or friends. Many times your personal savings will be used to get started. Later, an investor may take a favorable view of your project. Your investment, of course, contains the risk that you may lose your money and end up deeply in debt to family and friends. Nothing ruins solid relationships faster.

Banks — While most banks will not lend to new ventures, some are willing to lend money to small businesses to finance fixed assets, inventories, and accounts receivable where substantial collateral is available. Some banks even have venture capital subsidiaries that operate in essentially the same manner as private venture capital firms.

Government Lending Programs — The Small Business Administration (SBA) provides financing to small business through direct loans or loan guarantees made to private lending institutions. To obtain a list of your local banks which are approved SBA centers, visit the library or consult your local telephone directory for the phone number of the local SBA office.

Government Grant Programs — One good way to receive funds for new idea development is when the idea also serves a need for the government. Through the SBA, Office of Innovation, Research and Technology, you can receive SBIR Pre-Solicitation Announcements. If you qualify as a small business, you can receive grants for research and development through the U.S. Department of Defense, Department of Commerce, Department of Energy, Department of Health and Human Services, or the Environmental Protection Agency. In general, the solicitation includes a list of problems that these federal agencies wish to solve, and allows you to submit a proposal for researching the solution.

The three-phase program grants up to $50,000 in the first phase, up to $500,000 in the second phase, and phase three is conducted by nonfederal funds to take the solution to commercial applications.

For further information and to be included on the government's mailing list, write to:

Office of Innovation, Research and Technology
U.S. Small Business Administration
1441 L Street, NW
Washington, DC 20416
(202) 653-7875 in Washington, DC
(214) 767-7643 in Dallas, Texas

Other sources of information regarding SBIR grants include:

The Small Business High Technology Institute
3300 North Central Avenue, Suite 1700
Phoenix, AZ 85012
(602) 277-6603
Provides a report to the states and a collection of successful Phase 1 proposals.

The Innovation Development Institute
45 Beach Bluff Avenue, Suite 300
Swampscott, MA 01907-0195
(617) 595-2920

Offers a newsletter entitled Inknowvation, telephone information services, and orientation seminars.

Peat, Marwick, Main and Company
700 First Oklahoma Tower
Oklahoma City, OK 73102
(405) 239-6411

Has available a concise proposal-writing booklet entitled Small Business Innovation Research Grants: How to Obtain Them to Finance Your Ideas. Consulting services are also provided for a fee

Sandra Conn Associates, Inc.
Suite 400
2551 North Clark Street
Chicago, IL 60614-1717
(312) 327-0082

A proposal writing book entitled Writing SBIR Proposals, plus orientation and proposal-writing seminars.

Other Forms of Financing

Private or exempt public offerings — While an unlikely source for immediate start-up capital, a company in an expansion phase may be able to raise capital for promoting new products without fully registering its offering with the Securities and Exchange Commission (SEC) or similar state commissions. One should consider such factors as lag time between initiation and actual financing, and the complexities of having private shareholders.

Registered Public Offering — A full-scale registration with the SEC and state authorities may be required when seeking larger amounts of capital. As with private placements, most small ventures will not view public offerings as an attractive financing source due to the time, cost, and registration requirements involved.

Venture Capitalists

Venture capital firms are usually privately owned or formed as general or limited partnerships, composed primarily of institutional investors or wealthy individuals. Most venture capital firms will seek investments in which they expect to realize a high rate of return – many times 10 to 1 or higher.

Whatever source of funding you choose will depend largely upon your own situation and knowledge or background.

One consideration which may be overlooked is the importance of understanding your state and federal securities laws on fund raising efforts. When dealing with friends and relatives, an inventor may forget that any efforts to raise capital require compliance with state and federal securities laws. Check with your legal adviser.

Some sources for finding venture capital include:

National Venture Capital Association (NVCA)
1225 19th Street NW, Suite 750
Washington, DC 20036
(202) 659-5756

National Association of Small Business Investment Companies (NASBIC)
618 Washington Building NW
Washington, DC 20005
(202) 638-3411

Venture Capital Hotline
(800) 237-2380
There is a $75 cost for this service.

Office of Energy Related Inventions
(a division of the National Bureau of Standards)
Department of Commerce
Gaithersburg, MD 20899
Provides grants for research and development.

National Science Foundation (NSF)
1800 G Street, NW
Washington, DC 20550
Provides federal research and development funding.

Starting Your Own Business

Going into business to manufacture and sell your invention is a major undertaking that involves more time, money, and energy than most people imagine. It is also very risky. Every new enterprise begins with optimism and enthusiasm, but less than 25% survive the first year. Many more go out of business the second year, and yet the few that do succeed and grow become an inspiration to future entrepreneurs. It takes dedication and diligence.

Starting and operating a business will involve, at the minimum, decisions on organizational options, management style, accounting techniques, marketing approach, legal and tax fundamentals, insurance planning, and many other considerations.

Just filling out the tax forms can make many would-be business people reconsider going into business. But, if you consider these matters as only part of the adventure, your dedication will generally pay off.

Describing the day-to-day operation of a business could easily fill a book. An excellent source for such information is PSI Research/ The Oasis Press, which publishes the *Starting and Operating a Business* series. The series consists of a separate book for each of the 50 states and the District of Columbia. Each book contains detailed information on federal and state laws and tax rates, and includes checklists and worksheets to help you get your business off to the right start. The books are available at book stores and some libraries.

Incubators

If you wish to start your own business, and promote and manufacture your own product, you should consider a business incubator.

The small business incubator is an increasingly popular and innovative economic development tool to improve the success rate of new firms. An incubator is a building or group of buildings in which a number of new or growing businesses can locate and operate with much lower overhead cost than in a conventional space where rent would be much higher.

Incubator facilities are characterized by access to shared, centralized services such as clerical and administrative help, receiving and shipping facilities, conference rooms, computers, fax and copy machines, and assistance. Because the incubator is designed to promote the development of small businesses, it provides low-cost space, business counseling and training, and a co-op environment offering expertise and information to its tenants.

Many of the 200-plus incubator projects across the nation have been sponsored by private corporations interested in new product development and services. Many small companies starting out in an incubator get that extra edge to help them survive the first few years when mistakes can be all too costly.

The SBA's Division of Management Assistance sponsors nationwide assistance programs, including the Small Business Development Center (SBDC) program for small businesses. There are more than 500 universities and colleges participating in this program. By calling the toll-free number below, you may find that using an advisor is to your benefit. They may be contacted at:

Division of Management Assistance
Small Business Administration
1441 L Street NW
Washington, DC 20410
(800) 368-5855

NOTES

NOTES

_____

_____

_____

_____

_____

_____

_____

_____

_____

_____

_____

_____

_____

_____

_____

_____

_____

_____

_____

_____

_____

_____

_____

_____

Chapter 7

Licensing

Your invention's evolution – from concept to market – involves substantial time, money, and effort. You are responsible for taking an idea and turning it into something of value, and you may look to licensing to reward your efforts.

The first step in licensing is, of course, finding someone who is interested in your idea or product. Finding a licensee is much like many of the other steps in developing your idea. You must decide what you want, research your prospects, then go after it. Your chance of licensing your idea will depend greatly upon how well you've completed each development and marketing stage.

If you are presently marketing your idea, even in a limited fashion, your idea has much greater merit, and you may have had inquiries already from your competitors about licensing arrangements.

The best place to start looking for a licensee is within the industry with which your product is associated. The *Thomas Register* is an excellent source for names. Generally, the process of writing letters to prospective licensees can take time. If you have not done any marketing, it may be time to start publicizing that your product is up for license, as well as approaching your business contacts.

The local Chamber of Commerce and business support centers will also provide leads. Contacting local venture capitalists or banks can also provide possibilities; however, local interests are generally much easier to deal with.

Remember, industry needs new products. It is a matter of being seen by those seeking something innovative.

Inventors are usually at their most vulnerable at this point. Be careful in thinking that the first interested party will be your last. As the inventor, you probably feel as though you've come too far to miss the boat now, and you may make a hasty decision in signing a contract, just to say you've done it. Try not to get too excited, feeling as though you're lucky just to have someone talking to you. On the other hand, realize it is the licensee who is taking the risk and adjust accordingly.

Preliminary Considerations

Before finding a prospective licensee or going to the table to negotiate a licensing agreement, you should be aware of what you want. Many inventors find license negotiations very intimidating and may lose certain bargaining points because of their inexperience.

Before any negotiating takes place, consider these points:

- Royalty percentage: Five percent is generally a good starting point for the the inventor receiving up-front money as well.

- Up-front money: A strong bargaining point and possible trade-off potential for higher royalties.

- Legal assistance: A lawyer may be well worth his or her pay during negotiations.

- Trust: Do you really trust the company you're dealing with? What is its background?

- Involvement: Do you want or need to be involved after the deal is signed?

Finding a Licensee

If you have a truly unique product, licensing can be as simple as going to the store aisles where your competitors' products are found. Companies are always eager to expand their product lines into new areas, or to sell improved versions of currently available products. Nearly every package gives the name and location of its producer.

After visiting the store, go to the library and become familiar with the sources available for research. The best sources for investigating licensing include:

Dun & Bradstreet's Reference Book of Corporate Management, which gives a detailed biographical description of more than 75,000 principal officers of more than 12,000 leading companies. It supplies names, titles, and an array of vital statistics.

Standard & Poor's Register of Corporations, Directors and Executives, which lists 45,000 corporations along with their executives and detailed information on some 450,000 potential licensee contacts.

Other good sources are the *Million Dollar Directory* and the *Middle Market Directory*, both from Dun & Bradstreet, listing thousands of companies, each with assets exceeding $500,000.

It is important to note that communications with a potential licensee should be directed to top management – the president or chief executive officer. Although letters are many times first screened by secretaries, professional-looking communications will almost always draw attention to your and your product. Remember the tips on appearing professional.

You will, unfortunately, receive your share of "we're not interested" letters. But for now, just put them aside for future reference.

Meeting with a Potential Licensee

A successful first meeting with a potential licensee is crucial to your licensing effort – you are not only promoting your product, you are also promoting yourself as knowledgeable and professional. The following are some points you should be prepared to cover:

1. Describe the demand for the product and how you know about the demand. Include market research and testing.

2. Discuss all the applications and alternatives to the product.

3. Demonstrate why the licensee will benefit from your product, and discuss the innovation presently on the market.

4. Discuss potential patents, trademarks, and copyrights.

5. Explain your qualifications for inventing the product, emphasizing your business background.

Evaluating Your Contract

A sound licensing agreement will benefit both you and the licensee, but it's only as good as the integrity of those who sign it. Don't forget to read the fine print – if it looks too good to be true, it usually is.

Glossary of Terms Used in Contracts and Licenses

Become familiar with the legal definitions of terms commonly used in licensing and contracts. Understanding these terms now may help you protect your ideas and avoid lawsuits later.

Derivative Works — This refers to any refinement or modification to your product. If not properly defined, an improvement on your product could become their product, not yours, to license. Many contracts are weak in this area, and it is your responsibility to assure that any product improvement made by others is included in your product and that the altered product remains your property.

Gross Profits — This is the net sales price less the cost of raw materials, labor, manufacturing, shipping, and packaging. Many different costs may be subtracted from the gross profits. Be very careful about labor cost, because a manufacturer or investor can take back all that he invested in the product and take a tax write-off. This costing must be defined and controlled now, or your royalties may pay the investor's brother $100,000 a year to box the product.

Licensed Devices — This explains exactly what the invention consists of and limits the scope of the agreement to only that product. Look to the future; you may be in another business later and may want to license to another industry.

Licensed Patents — This includes the patent number and claims, or gives an explanation beyond that detailed under Licensed Devices. If a patent is pending, detail what happens if you are not granted a patent, because it could happen.

Term — This is the amount of time the license will run.

Performance Clause — This could be the most important definition included. A performance clause will simply state a minimum number of units which should be sold within a specified period of time. It works well as an "anti-shelving" clause and it should explain in detail what happens if sales performance is not met. The anti-shelving clause is a means of keeping interest in your product, as the licensee will be paying royalties to you even if the product never reaches the market. After a certain time, all rights should revert back to you. If this is not clearly set out in writing, you will have to go to court to win your invention back.

Payment — Detail how much is paid to you and to others, and when. It should include a late penalty and a time limit for payments or royalties, and should detail what happens when payments are not met. You should include a cut-off point for late payments where all rights revert back to you and a statement that any partial payments are nonrefundable.

Records and Reports — Define the type of records to be kept, and also allow for an independent audit, which helps keep everyone honest. It should also indicate whether the investor is entitled to review records which can be important in estimating royalties.

Research and Development — This defines the effort to stay ahead of the competition and should even include fees to be paid to the inventor for further research.

Third Party Infringement — This can cause much hardship and it must be detailed as to who fights the lawsuits. The licensee will consider it the inventor's problem, yet the business could fail if the inventor is poorly financed. Be careful of the wording.

Sublicensing — This can be a quick way for the inventor to lose all control if not restricted by the original contract. If the contract does not restrict sublicensing, you could find yourself competing with your own product shipped from another country.

Termination and Abandonment — This specifies what happens if everything falls through. Make sure that in a licensing agreement you have no responsibility to pay back company loans. State clearly that you receive all rights to improvements should the contract fail.

Minimum Royalty — This details the minimum amount of royalty you will receive at certain intervals. It should say you will get paid, no matter what problems the licensee may encounter.

Up-Front Payment — Negotiating for up-front money will depend largely upon the product and how badly the licensee wants it. I have signed deals where as much as $50,000 was paid up front, so it can be done. The licensee may argue that he has to invest in molds, engineering, testing, and start-up. Your argument of course, is that the money is required to reimburse out-of-pocket expenses for development, prototyping, patenting, and other costs. Additionally, up-front money will sometimes make the licensee work a little harder to recoup his or her investment.

Exclusivity — National or even worldwide exclusivity rights can be a strong negotiating position and should not be bargained away easily. Use exclusivity as a bargaining chip and remember, if you found one licensee, you can find more.

While negotiating a licensing agreement for your invention, it pays to stay cool and view things from all possible angles. Taking time to think now will help you avoid licensing what could result in a future lawsuit. Litigation could take years to be settled and it will cost you more than is imaginable before you recover any money, if ever.

Due to the complexity of the subject, only a few legal considerations of licensing have been discussed. It is always advisable to look into local and state restrictions when signing any legal document. Many inventors will fall into unfamiliar territory when negotiating a license and could fail to follow local or state antitrust and securities laws. Legal counsel should seriously be considered when getting ready to sign on the dotted line.

Some organizations which deal with licensing issues include:

The National Venture Capital Association (NVCA)
1225 19th Street NW, Suite 750
Washington, DC 20036
(202) 659-5756

The National Association of Small Business Investment Companies (NASBIC)
618 Washington Building NW
Washington DC 20005
(202) 638-3411

Licensing Industry Merchandisers' Association
200 Park Avenue, Suite 303E
New York, NY 10166

Some magazines which will carry licensing articles include:

Invention Management
85 Irving Street
Arlington, MA 02174

Product Design and Development
Chilton Company
Chilton Way
Radnor, PA 19089

International New Product Newsletter
6 St. James Avenue
Boston, MA 02116

International Invention Register Catalyst
P.O. Box 547
Fallbrook, CA 92028

In Business
The JG Press
P.O. Box 323
18 South Seventh Street
Emmaus, PA 18049

Industrial Research and Development Magazine
Technical Publishing
1301 South Grove Street
Barrington, IL 60010

The Licensing Agreement

The following license agreement is an example of a contract favoring the inventor. It may help you in comparing with others which may lean toward the licensee.

This contract is a guide. As with the tax laws, state and federal securities laws, and other laws which impact on business, licensing may be subject to state and federal franchise laws, antitrust laws, and case law. To be safe, check with your legal adviser.

License Agreement

This agreement is made between

_____ ("Licensor") and

_____ ("Licensee")

on _____, 19 ____. Licensor is the sole inventor and owner of

_____ ("Intellectual Property")

including but not limited to certain information, technical data, processes, know-how, stop practices, drawings, plans, specifications, methods of manufacture, trademarks, and other data herein after known as the invention. Licensee desires to obtain a nonexclusive license to utilize the information and to manufacture and sell the invention. In consideration of the mutual promises in this agreement, the parties agree as follows and defined herein:

1. Scope. This agreement shall be limited to the product and information known as the invention.

2. License. Subject to the terms of this agreement, Licensor grants to Licensee the nonexclusive, nontransferable right and license to use the information to manufacture the invention and sell or lease the invention within the United States. No license, expressed or implied, is granted to employ the information for any other purpose whatsoever.

3. Compensation.

   A. Payment. The consideration due and payable to Licensor for the rights granted to Licensee hereunder shall be the sum of $_____ U.S. dollars due and payable on execution of this agreement.

   B. Further Consideration. As further consideration for the grants of this license provides for hereunder, Licensee agrees to spend no less than $_____ for the purpose of manufacturing, distribution and promotion of the invention before 6 months from the date of execution of this agreement.

  C. Royalties. In addition to the consideration due and payable to Licensor, Licensee agrees to assume and pay royalties on all licensed devices sold equal to _____% of the gross profits realized from the exploration and rights to the licensed invention.

  D. Payment Schedule. After _____ 19____. Payments of royalties shall be paid to Licensor with each quarterly report.

4. Records. Licensee shall maintain accurate records relating to the manufacturing and sale of the invention. Licensee shall render quarterly reports to Licensor within three weeks of the end of each quarter showing the total quantity of inventions produced; the quantity sold, leased or otherwise utilized; the gross receipts received by Licensor for such transactions; and the amounts due Licensor as royalties. Licensor or an authorized representative shall have the right to inspect and copy such records and books of account upon Licensor's written request, and such inspection and copying shall be done during Licensee's regular business hours.

5. Research and Development. Licensee shall make funds available for the further research, development and improvements and derivative works of the invention. Funds shall be no less than $_____ per year. All improvements and derivative works of the invention shall be included within this agreement.

6. Termination of the agreement.

  A. Unless terminated sooner, this agreement shall remain in force through _____, 19_____.

  B. Either party shall have the right to terminate this agreement if the other fails to perform per written agreement herein, provided that such failure shall not have been remedied by the defaulting party within sixty days of having received written notice of intention to terminate.

  C. Bankruptcy or Insolvency of Licensee shall automatically terminate this agreement with all rights returning to Licensor.

D. Licensee shall have the right to sell or lease any products on hand or contracted for as of the date of termination. Any termination shall not release Licensee from payment of royalties accrued through the date of termination.

7. This agreement shall be interpreted in accordance with the laws of the State of _____.

8. Licensee agrees to make adequate warning for the product, and comply with all applicable laws and regulations.

9. Licensee agrees to carry third party liability insurance to insure and adequately cover both Licensor and Licensee against claims resulting from damage or personal injury through sale or use of the product (Invention). Licensee agrees to make Licensor as an additional insured on such insurance policies.

10. No terms of this agreement can be modified or waived except in writing signed by both parties.

11. Service of notice as provided for in this agreement shall be given in writing and shall be considered duly served and given by mailing the same, postage prepaid by registered mail to the parties at the following addresses:

_____
_____
_____

and

_____
_____
_____

12. A minimum royalty shall be paid to Licensor of $_____ per month for the first 6 months after execution of agreement and $_____ per month from 7th month on.

13. Licensee shall permit, during normal business hours, a duly authorized representative of the Licensor, or Licensor to enter Licensee premises for purpose of ascertaining that the Licensee is complying with the provisions of this agreement.

14. Nothing herein shall be construed as a warranty or representation given by Licensor to Licensee attesting to the scope or validity of the herein named patent application or any patent issuing thereon.

15. Third Party Infringement suits shall be entered into equally with Licensor monies transferred from future royalties if necessary. Said settlement shall be equally divided between Licensee and Licensor.

In witness whereof the parties hereto have hereunto signed their respective names and affixed their respective corporate seal.

_____ ("Licensor")

_____ ("Licensee")

Executed this _____ day of _____, 19 _____

NOTES

Bibliography

The One Minute Manager
By Kenneth Blanchard and Spencer Johnson
Berkley Books, New York, 1982

Guerrilla Marketing
By Jay Conrad Levinson
Houghton Miffin Company, Boston, 1984

New Product Development Strategies
By Frederick Buggie
AMACOM, New York, 1981

Business Services and Information: The Guide to the Federal Government.
Management Information Exchange, Philadelphia, 1978

National Trade and Professional Associations of the U.S.
Columbia Books, Inc., Washington, D.C., 1987

Business Information Sources
By Lorna M. Daniells
University of California Press, Berkeley, Calif., 1985

Trade Shows and Professional Exhibits Directory
By Robert Elster
Gale Research Company, Detroit, 1985

Federal Government Directory of Information Resources in the U.S.
U.S. Government Printing Office, Washington, D.C., 1974

The Patent Book
By James Gregory and Kevin Mulligan
A & W Publishers, New York, 1979

New Product Development
By George Gruenwald
NTC Business Books, Lincolnwood, Ill., 1985

Inventors' Source Book
By Susan Hartman and Norman Parrish
Inventors Resource Center Publishers, Berkeley, Calif., 1978

A Handbook for Inventors
By Calvin MacCrachen
Scribner's, New York, 1983

Manual of Patent Examining Procedures
U.S. Department of Commerce, Patent & Trademark Office,
Washington, D.C., 1989

The Inventors Handbook
By Robert Park
Betterway Publications, White Hall, Virginia, 1986

Patent It Yourself
By David Pressman
Nolo Press, Berkeley, Calif., 1989

Standard & Poor's Industry Surveys
Standard & Poor, Inc., New York, 1989

The Guide to Venture Capital Sources
Capital Publishing, Wellesley Hills, Mass.

Finding Facts Fast: How to Find Out What You Want and Need to Know
By Alden Todd
Ten Speed Press, Berkeley, Calif., 1979

Products and Markets
By William H. Reynolds
Appleton-Century-Crofts/Meredith, New York, 1969

Writing the Natural Way
By Gabriele Lusser Rico
Tarcher, Los Angeles, 1983

Why Didn't I Think of That!
By Robert L. Shook
New American Library, New York, 1982

How to Cash in on Your Bright Ideas!
By George G. Siposs
Universal Development, Orange, Calif., 1980

The Sources of Invention
By John Jewkes, David Sawyers and Richard Stillerman
Norton, New York, 1969

The Insiders Guide to Small Business Resources
By David E. Gumpert and Jeffry A. Timmons
Doubleday, Garden City, New York, 1982

Why Did They Name It…?
By Hannah Campbell
Fleet, New York, 1964

Copyright Basics
Copyright Office, Library of Congress, Washington, D.C.

Small Business Guide to Federal R & D Funding Opportunities
Dept. of Energy, Assistant General for Patents, Washington, D.C.

The Disclosure Document Program,
General Information Concerning Patents
General Information Concerning Trademarks
Guide for Patent Draftsmen
Official Gazette of the United States Patent and Trademark Office,
Patent Profiles
Patent and Trademark Office, Washington, D.C.

Index